WHY JESUS NEVER HAD ULCERS

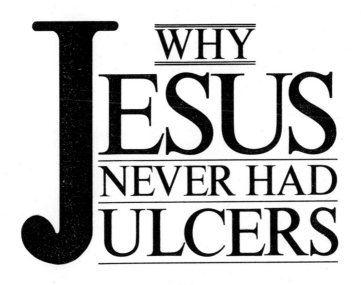

WHY JESUS NEVER HAD ULCERS

&

Other Thought-Provoking Questions

Robert M. Holmes

ABINGDON PRESS / NASHVILLE

TO

Dr. RONALD E. SLEETH

my professor of preaching and best man
at my wedding

WHY JESUS NEVER HAD ULCERS

Library of Congress Cataloging-in-Publication Data

Holmes, Robert M. (Robert Merrill), 1925–
    Why Jesus never had ulcers and other thought-
    provoking questions.

    Bibliography: p.
    1. Methodist Church—Sermons. 2. United Meth-
odist Church (U.S.)—Sermons. 3. Sermons, Ameri-
can. I. Title.
BX8333.H585W48 1986   252'.076   85-30640

ISBN 0-687-45359-3

This book is printed on acid-free paper.

MANUFACTURED BY THE PARTHENON PRESS AT
NASHVILLE, TENNESSEE, UNITED STATES OF AMERICA

Contents

INTRODUCTION

TO LIVE is to choose. Someone has said that from the moment a baby first discovers that it can't "holler and swaller at the same time," life is a series of choices.

This is especially true of the Christian, and Jesus is forever reminding us of it. "You cannot serve two masters," he says. On a more disturbing note he tells us, "He who loves father or mother . . . son or daughter more than me is unworthy of me." What he's asking is "Who is first with you? There cannot be more than one."

Questions such as these make the Christian pilgrimage so difficult. We are confronted with choices we wish we didn't have to make; therefore, we often postpone them or neglect them altogether. But, as we have often been reminded, "Not to decide is to decide."

On the other hand, there are some choices a Christian is *not* called to make, choices that we often, erroneously, think we must make. One of these is the presumed choice between being Christian and being intelligent. When Jesus specified as the fundamental law of life, "Love the Lord your God with all your heart, and with all your soul, and with all your strength, and with all your mind; and your neighbor as yourself" (Luke 10:27), he quite explicitly and intentionally included loving God with the *mind.* That is not to say that faith is limited to reason; it is to say that faith is not the enemy of reason. One need not—indeed, one should not—park one's brains at the sanctuary door when one enters, or for that matter, when one leaves.

This is what makes preaching and listening to sermons such hard work sometimes. A good sermon requires good thinking on the part of both the preacher and the listener. That means receiving a sermon with an open mind, which is important as long as it isn't open at both ends. As G. K. Chesterton said, "The purpose of an open mind, like that of an open mouth, is to close on something solid." One need not choose between being a person of faith and being a person of intellect.

Another choice some mistakenly feel they have to make is between spirituality and social involvement. This illusory division is probably the principal cause for fracture within the church today. Those caught in this dichotomy can even drift into the misperception that social action is the enemy of true Christian witness, or that spirituality is the enemy of service. The church today needs to do all it can to overcome this schism. We might well paraphrase the famous quote in which John Wesley decried the faulty split between "knowledge and vital piety" by saying, "The time has come to join together those two so long divided: social action and spirituality."

A third choice is more obviously fraudulent, and that's the choice between loving God, loving self, and loving neighbor. To be sure, there is a clear priority to this three-part law, but it is a matter of spiritual and psychological sequence. Before we can genuinely love our neighbors and be in good relationship with them, we must love and be in good relationship with ourselves, and before that is possible, we must be receptive and responsive to God. This sequence is as natural and undeniable as the fact that a parent loves his baby before the baby can love anyone. As we grow in our love for God, we become better able to love ourselves and others. To choose one object of love, to the exclusion of another, is neither rational nor Christian.

So, it is in this context of choices, some of which must be acknowledged as inevitable while others are identified as spurious, that these messages are set. My hope is that they will provoke deeper thought; perhaps, even richer life. In an era of personal confusion, social turmoil, pain and brokenness, these messages attempt to lift up a Christ who is a model for facing choices. This age, like every age, is "the best of times and the worst of times." It is also a time of unlimited possibility. The fulfillment of that possibility begins with a deepening of spirit, a sharpening of mind, a broadening of social sensitivity, a faithful confidence in the capabilities of a loving and obedient disciple in the service of a powerful and gracious God, and a zeal to move beyond all false choices to the final choice: for whom shall we live our lives?

These sermons were preached on "The Protestant Hour" in 1986 and before that to the congregation of St. Paul's United Methodist Church in Helena, Montana. I wish to thank Dr. David Abernathy, executive director of the United Methodist Joint Communications Committee, for his warm and supportive assistance to me in this broadcasting and publishing venture.

Special thanks are due to my editor-daughter, Krys, whose professional skills were gently applied to these sermons for publication, and to Pam Younghans for typing and correcting the final manuscripts. Most indispensible of all has been the loving and consistent encouragement of my wife, Polly Mudge Holmes.

Helena, Montana
September 2, 1985

ONE

Why Jesus Never Had Ulcers

Scripture: Psalm 23;
Matthew 6:25-34

I HAVE a friend who once expressed two fears. One fear was that if he did not slow down he could have a heart attack. The other fear was that if he didn't hurry up, he would not be able to accomplish enough that was useful before he had his heart attack.

I'm told that Americans consume 97 percent of the world's aspirin. Heart attacks and peptic ulcers are hitting more people, and hitting them sooner, than ever before in our country. A lot of folks have ulcers already and many more may be on their way to having them. Jesus never had them, and as followers of his, perhaps we'd better pause long enough to ask why.

I've heard several explanations. Some say he never lived long enough to get them. One person said he didn't have six children and an ailing wife. Another person explains that he didn't have to repay the national debt or keep drug pushers out of the neighborhood. It's true that Jesus lived in a time that was quite different from ours. The pace was not as fast nor the competition as keen, perhaps. People did not strive for more; they settled for less. Without newscasts every hour, they weren't encumbered with the world's problems in addition to their own. Life was relatively simple and the lifespan relatively short.

In other words, there were not as many ulcer producers

in that ancient Palestinian culture as there are today. But do not underestimate the tensions that surrounded Jesus. He didn't retire from carpentering on a pension. He noted that birds have nests and foxes have holes but the Son of man had no place to lay his head. He often had no guarantees about the next meal or the next night's lodging. Moreover, he was trying to fulfill an impossible assignment—to bring in a kingdom, or at least start a movement, without benefit of clergy or army or political pull. In fact, he was pretty promptly identified as being in quite a separate camp from clergy, army, or government. And underlying all of this was the prospect of an early end to his earthly life.

In spite of the differences between his culture and ours, Jesus of Nazareth knew pressures that you and I have never known. Yet he never had ulcers. Why? The answer does not lie in anything that was unique about his physiological makeup or any advantage he may have had that we do not have. The answer lies, rather, in resources available to all of us of which Jesus was willing to take advantage.

To begin with, Jesus never lost his perspective about himself, his work, where he fit into things, and what did and did not depend on him. To gain a proper perspective, whether it be of a painting or of your life's work, you must stand back for a time and set yourself apart in order to get a broader, fuller look. Jesus had to retreat time and again, and we must do the same.

The real purpose of a retreat is not just to "get away from it all" but to get a better view. It's not so much like hiding in a cave, where you can see nothing, as it is climbing a mountain, where you can see the entire landscape, where you can ask, How is everything fitting together and where am I fitting into the scheme? This is where a contemplative monk, cloistered in his monastery, may miss the force of Jesus' message. It is not hard to retreat from a world of struggle and conflict. It's a cinch to find peace of mind when you are divorced from the world. The challenge lies in keeping peace of mind when you are *in* the world.

The purpose of the retreats you and I experience periodically (vacations, "nights out," long weekends, a walk in the park, "spiritual renewal weekends," etc.) is to help us regain perspective, to see ourselves more properly in relation to the world around us and to God, and to recharge our spiritual batteries with power to meet the challenges that lie around us.

A certain tuba player in the philharmonic orchestra, so the tale goes, got a night off because he had had a tooth pulled. He decided to come to the concert and sit in the audience for a change. He took his seat in the front row of the balcony where he could see and hear everything. He was thrilled with what he heard, and afterward he ran backstage to his comrades and shouted, "You know what? The symphony doesn't go 'oompah, oompah, oompah' at all!" For the first time, he had seen himself in relation to the entire symphony.

It is easy to get obsessed with our indispensability. I've known some busy mothers who have had the liberating experience of having to go to the hospital for a few days and later discovering that the family got along just fine. The family need not foster a dependency but can be a partnership. This can be an important discovery for the entire family. Or your experience may be more like mine. When you come back to your own job after having been gone awhile, you may find you really haven't been missed, and that things have run quite smoothly without you. We all need to learn, occasionally, that we have a valuable contribution to make, but that the world does not rest on our shoulders.

Getting away sometimes helps us to see problems in their proper perspective. Many years ago a certain newspaper carried at the top of its editorial column these lines:

> Some of your hurts you have cured,
>   And the sharpest you still have survived;
> But what torments of grief you've endured
>   From the evils that never arrived.

Jesus said simply, "Do not be anxious about tomorrow, for tomorrow will be anxious for itself. Let the day's own trouble be sufficient for the day" (Matt. 6:34). This much of Jesus' formula for avoiding ulcers is nothing new to us. But how do you just relax in the midst of deadlines, keen competition, heavy schedules, and frightening world problems?

The second part of Jesus' secret for avoiding ulcers is not as obvious as the first. Jesus was not afraid to fail. And you know, I think most of us are. Success has become a byword in our culture. Everyone must succeed. Graduating classes even try to predict who is most likely to do so. Recent tests among college students indicate that more than half of them put financial success as their number one goal in life.

Jesus, on the other hand, seemed not at all concerned about being a "success." During the forty-day interval in the wilderness after his baptism, he tried to get a careful understanding of his mission in life, and he rejected three specific forms of success—fame, wealth, and power. From that time on he refused to be dismayed by people's disappointment in him. First the hierarchy scoffed; then John the Baptist became disillusioned; his own family questioned his choices; and finally even his disciples grew skeptical. Jesus was considered a failure by nearly everyone on earth whose opinion meant a lot to him.

Apparently Jesus never lost any sleep over this, though many of us would have. There is practically nothing we would rather avoid than to be considered a failure in the eyes of our fellow human beings—professionally, financially, or socially. I suspect more ulcers are generated by the single human drive for success than by any other cause. This drive can fool us. We are a good deal more concerned about keeping up with the Joneses than we think we are. We want to provide for our families—for their sakes, of course, and we don't want to do a less adequate job of it than the Joneses do. What the economist Thorstein Veblen long ago called "conspicuous consumption" is a means of showing the world—particularly the Joneses—just how successful we really are.

Parental problems, more often than not, involve the fear of what others will think. Concern about my teenager and the places he goes, or concern about my four-year-old who hasn't stopped sucking his thumb, or my toddler who expresses his anger in public, is complicated by my more unconscious concern for what people will think of me as a parent.

Well, Jones never bothered Jesus. At no time did Jesus ever define his course of action on the basis of what people expected of him, and he tried to free us from this worry as well. It is God's expectation that counts.

Jesus said that if you labor in trust, God will see to your basic needs, but don't be anxious about your life, what you shall eat, what you shall put on. Life is a whole lot more than that! We may not get rich, we may not become famous, we may not gain power, but life is more than that, and if we live in trust, God will provide us with all that is required for a full and meaningful life.

There is an art to failing successfully, it seems to me—in accepting the fact that we may not only *appear* to fail in some things, we *will* fail in some things. We cannot be all things to all people. We have to choose where we are willing to fail for the sake of succeeding elsewhere.

A homemaker may have to choose between being a meticulous housekeeper, or even an award-winning church worker, and being a good parent. A provider may have to choose between earning extra money outside the home and being present more often with the family. I have known some people who, looking back, wished they had settled for a cheaper *house* in order to have a more joyous *home*. A minister, a teacher, a person in public service, and many others, whose work, like an iceberg, is largely unseen, constantly face the choice between doing what needs to be done and doing what will look good to onlookers. They also must make choices among many good projects that cannot all be completed in the time available. One cannot save the entire world before the children get home from school.

Jesus was the most conscientious person who ever lived, but he was not, thank God, a perfectionist. In fact, it's remarkable how disorganized his efforts appear to have been. As far as establishing a movement was concerned, or starting a revolution, he didn't organize anything. He just went on from day to day, loving and serving and listening. The perfection of his life was in his love, and nothing else. This is the perfection toward which we are called to strive, with the assurance that repentance for failure to love well enough brings, with forgiveness, a power to love better. We have every reason to seek this kind of perfection (or, as Jesus put it, to "seek his kingdom and his righteousness"). But if, in anything else, you are a perfectionist, you may be on your way to an ulcer—something Jesus never had.

One more reason Jesus never had an ulcer: He never forgot who was in charge. He refused to shoulder more responsibility than was properly his. This is one of our most common sins. It has been well said that one of the finest arts of the religious life is "letting go and letting God." At this art Jesus was indeed a master. He seemed

16

to know the meaning of Reinhold Niebuhr's famous "Prayer for Serenity."

> O God, grant us the serenity to accept
> What cannot be changed;
> The courage to change what can be changed,
> And the wisdom to know the one from the
>   other.

Jesus never forgot who was in charge. He bore unmeasured burdens, he faced extreme temptations, he confronted insurmountable obstacles, he was mercilessly treated, but he never forgot who was in charge.

When we feel as though we are faced with burdens that do not lighten, or have lost too many battles ourselves, it is not because God's strength has failed us; it may be because we do not see the whole picture, or it may be that God's timing is different from ours. F. W. Faber has reminded us of the importance of keeping step with God. He says:

> We must wait for God, long, meekly, in the wind and the wet, in the thunder and lightning, in the cold and dark. Wait and God will come. God never comes to those who do not wait . . . When he comes, go with Him, but go slowly, fall a little behind, and when He quickens His pace, be sure of it before you quicken yours. But when He slackens, slacken at once and so not be slow only, but silent, very silent, for He is God.[1]

Peace of mind, in this sense, is more than just relaxing. Jesus didn't say, "Forget it, it will all turn out." It's not that the hymn we often sing that speaks of "foes to vanquish" and "duties to perform" is wrong; it is just that it must always be sung with another truth in mind: that God will order the future as God has done the past, that God is on the side of the values that count the most.

Whoever knows this God of supreme power and perfect love and ultimate victory, is not just likely to avoid ulcers, but is certain to find abundant life.

Two

Prayer and a Rabbit's Foot

Scripture: John 14:8-14

I N HIS *Christmas Oratorio,* W. H. Auden included this strange prayer:

Oh God, put away justice and truth, for we cannot understand them and do not want them. Eternity would bore us dreadfully. Leave thy heavens and come down to our earth of waterclocks and hedges. Become our uncle. Look after baby, amuse grandfather . . . help Willy with his homework, introduce Muriel to a handsome naval officer. Be interesting and weak like us, and we will love you as we love ourselves.[1]

Like it or not, that probably comes close to the kind of praying a lot of people do—if they pray at all. It's interesting, and not just a little paradoxical, that such a thing as "prayer" can be thought of by some very intelligent people as one of the last vestiges of superstition, and yet of by other very intelligent people as a mystery of very real and transforming power.

And where do you come out on this? Where can any thinking person stand in a scientific and allegedly rational world in which we don't believe in ghosts and goblins but in which Christians are called upon to believe in prayer?

At one extreme is the thought that prayer is really no more and no less than the psychological lift one gets from talking to oneself. It clears the head and thus makes one aware of more options for action than had been thought of before. At the other extreme is the notion that prayer is a kind of magic device whereby if we pray hard enough, and get enough people to pray with us, we can somehow manipulate God into doing what we most want.

So at one extreme, prayer is simply positive thinking that helps us feel better. At the other, prayer has all the spiritual mechanics of a rabbit's foot. Now you know I'm going to say that the truth lies somewhere in between. You're right, but the starting point, at least for those of us who seek to follow Jesus Christ, must be in Christ's own words, which seem clear enough and are impossible to bend in any other direction: "Whatever you ask in my name, I will do it" (John 14:13).

On the surface, it almost sounds as if a prayer can become a good-luck charm that guarantees that whatever we want will be. But the surface of scripture, and particularly of Jesus' words, is never enough. Jesus said, "I have not come to bring peace, but a sword" (Matt. 10:34). And people have looked at the surface of that and have gone to war, thinking they were doing God's will. Jesus also said, "The poor you always have with you" (Matt. 26:11). People have looked at the surface of those words and decided God wanted them to do nothing about poverty and starvation. If we look at the surface of anything, all we see is a pleasing sheen, and in this Holy Book, that can mean deception, not by God's intention, but by our own inattention.

I know very little about prayer. And it isn't because I haven't prayed, because I have, in all kinds of ways, at all kinds of times, joyfully and apologetically. Yet I understand little about it. But I'll share with you out of my experience, and you may weigh it against your own experience, and your own praying. What I want to say is that prayer and a rabbit's foot are not the same thing at all, no matter how you and I may pray or mis-pray.

The first and most obvious difference is that any magical charm is a means of getting our own way, whereas prayer is a means of getting God's way. I say this is obvious, but perhaps it isn't. Perhaps the point at which we face the greatest danger of letting prayer become a rabbit's foot comes when we try to make prayer a means of manipulating God into doing our will. Remember Huckleberry Finn, reporting his first experience with prayer:

> Miss Watson she took me in the closet and prayed, but nothing come of it. She told me to pray every day, and whatever I asked for I would get it. But it warn't so. I tried it. Once I got a fish-line, but no hooks. It warn't any good to me without hooks. I tried for the hooks three or four times, but somehow I couldn't make it work. By-and-by, one day, I asked Miss Watson to try for me, but she said I was a fool. She never told me why, and I couldn't make it out no way.
>
> I set down, one time, back in the woods, and had a long think about it. I says to myself, if a body can get anything they pray for, why don't Deacon Winn get back the money he lost on pork? Why can't the widow get back her silver snuff-box that was stole? Why can't Miss Watson fat up? No, says I to myself, there ain't nothing in it.[2]

Huck Finn's experience was true enough, but his conclusion was wrong. When he said, "There ain't nothing in it," what he meant was that prayer is no way to guarantee you will get what you want, and he was right, but that is not what Christian prayer is all about. If prayer could be that kind of device in our hands, think what a hideous place this world would be! Dean William Inge has written: "If we think that we should like to control events by our prayers, let us consider how we should like the idea of our neighbor being able to control them by his. I once had a letter from a good lady who said, 'I am praying for your death. I have been very successful in two other cases.' "[3]

You see, the power of prayer could not be only lively but also deadly, if it automatically granted us divine ability to manipulate all happenings. But wait a minute. Jesus said, "Whatever you ask in my name, I will do it." Elsewhere he said, "Ask, and it will be given you; seek, and you will find; knock, and it will be opened to you. For every one who asks receives, and he who seeks finds, and to him who knocks it will be opened" (Matt. 7:7-8). Where is the difference between this and a rabbit's foot?

Looking beneath the surface of this requires we look not just at what Jesus said, but also at what he did. One of the ways in which Jesus is a model for me—and there are several—is in his own prayer life. He was absolutely direct in his prayer. He prayed out his frustration, his anger, even his despair, with God. When, after all the time they had spent together, one disciple said, "Lord show us the Father," Jesus must have known the meaning of frustration. And he didn't just swallow it; he prayed about it.

The essence of Jesus' own style of prayer is in that most agonizing and possibly longest prayer of his whole life, in Gethsemane. In that prayer, Jesus asked for what he wanted. He asked for his life. "If it be possible, let this cup pass from me," he said (Matt. 26:39), and he asked not once but several times. It was a prayer few of us on Earth have ever had to pray.

George Buttrick once said, "To pray is to expose oneself to the promptings of God." That must mean exposing completely one's desires and needs and feelings—and Jesus certainly did that. But he also took head-on the one part of prayer that gives it its power: He said, "Nevertheless not my will, but thine, be done."

Jesus meant what he prayed. He asked what he wanted, but at the same time he put himself at God's disposal. He asked to live, and within twenty-four hours he was dead.

21

He had made his will coincident with that of God. No rabbit's foot there. And perhaps you'd say, no victory, either—but it was too early to tell. It all points to the second meaning of prayer, and that has to do with responsibility.

There is a kind of praying, it seems to me, that leaves everything to God and nothing to humankind. It's the same kind of theology that grants God all the credit and humankind none at all. At best, that kind of praying is Pollyanna; at worst it is an escape. The Pollyanna is one who always sees a happy ending to everything. It's a romantic, an infantile kind of theology, which preaches that God can fix everything, mend every hurt, and will provide unending happiness. A touching sentiment, to be sure, but how honest? There are some breaks that cannot be mended, some mistakes that cannot be unwritten, some pains that are unavoidable.

I fear there are times we pray for God to do that which God has no intention of doing. There are times when we ask God to make a move when God is waiting for *us* to move—when we try to place upon God responsibility which God seeks to share with us.

I'm fond of the story of the time George Washington Carver was wanting to find more uses for the peanut, in order that the peanut-producing Southland might be freed from its economic havoc, and took his problem to God in prayer. He reported that God's answer to his prayer ran something like this: "George, I've given you hands and I've given you a brain. I've given you laws to use, and there is a microscope. Now go to it." This is not to say that in the last analysis prayer is a hoax and humankind is left on its own. It is to say what Augustine said long ago, that "without God's energy, man cannot; and without man's effort, God will not."

It is to say that our prayer requests must always be checked against God's own will, and because we are not always sure, we ask *in Jesus' name,* which means in his style, which is to say, "After all is said and done about what I wish and hope and want, nevertheless, not my will but thine be done," because I know it's infinitely better, even for me. Anything less is a rabbit's foot.

Finally, what this means to me is that one who prays, who asks what he will "in the name of Jesus," is willing to be open to unexpected answers. I believe God answers prayers in God's own way and in God's own time, as surely as God answered Jesus in Gethsemane, by granting him the capacity to do what he did not want to do at all. The question may be: Would we recognize an answer to prayer if we saw one—if, for example, the answer were "No," or "Wait," or something quite unexpected?

Perhaps the question going on in your head right now may be: "If prayer doesn't really make a difference anyway, why pray?" But I didn't say that prayer makes no difference. I think prayer makes a tremendous difference. I believe prayer is a power, and that whatever deficiency appears to exist lies not in that power but in our use of it.

What I mean is this: I take very seriously the idea that God created an unfinished world on purpose, and endowed us with certain gifts for helping to complete its creation. Intelligence is one of these gifts. Our intelligence is greater than we have ever discovered, certainly greater than we have used. It enables us to extend and multiply our physical capabilities a millionfold. We can think up things that will enable us to move mountains, fly faster than the speed of sound, see farther than the eye can see, and even photograph the development of a baby inside its mother's womb. I believe that just as our bodies and our minds can be instruments of enhancing the will of God on earth, so can our spiritual powers, about which we know so much less. I believe that, though I cannot explain it any more than a physicist can explain gravity or matter, or an astronomer can explain the calculable movements of the stars. My prayers for myself and others can be a way to participate in the working out of God's will, whether that be to bring peace, heal pain, or save a life.

Prayer does make a difference, and therefore I respect it quite as much as the powers of intellect or physical prowess. It is not a substitute for either, but a supplement to both. It is neither a ploy that leaves everything to us, nor an excuse to leave everything to God. It is one more means of the co-creation of this world to which we are called.

I know that not everything that happens is God's will, for God did create us free enough to violate his will from time to time, or postpone it. But I also know that real prayer is not a rabbit's foot, but rather a total exposure to the promptings of God *who helps us* make something new and redeemable out of every situation, something that, though God may not have planned it, can still be used to express God's will.

Meanwhile, "if your knees shake, fall on them"; for as someone has written, "Prayer has wrought more changes than this world dreams of."

THREE

Is the Golden Rule Really Christian?

Scripture: Jeremiah 22:1-9;
Matthew 7:1-12

TWENTY YEARS before the birth of Christ, two rabbis, Shammai and Hillel, were approached by a Gentile who asked them mockingly to teach them the whole law while standing on one foot. Now, everyone knew that the law of the Hebrew people filled many books (or scrolls, in those days), and to have read all of it could have taken several nights and days. Shammai became angry with the Gentile and told him to be on his way. But Hillel accepted the Gentile's challenge, and, as he stood on one foot, proceeded to teach what he considered to be the whole law: "Do not unto others," he said, "what you would not have others do unto you."

This was twenty years before Christ's birth: fifty years before he preached the Sermon on the Mount.

But it isn't only in the Jewish faith that we find what we think of as the Golden Rule. Interestingly enough, Confucius said, "Do not unto others what you would not they should do unto you." Buddhist writings include the statement, "Hurt no others with that which pains yourself." And Hinduism says, "Do naught to others which, if done to yourself, would cause you pain." Islam says, "No one of you is a believer until he loves for his brother what he loves for himself."

If the Golden Rule is Christian, it clearly isn't *exclusively* Christian. But that's not the point. I suggest that the Golden Rule, taken by itself, isn't really

Christian at all. I find many Christians who do take it by itself, and assume that this is what the Gospel is all about. When they do this, I think they miss the point entirely. Dr. Henry Hitt Crane, the famous pastor from Detroit, pointed out how much damage can be done by the Golden Rule if we take it literally. He said suppose your small child comes to you and asks for something he very much wants but is too young to handle without danger. Put yourself in the child's place. If you were a child and asked for a gun, or a hunting knife, or all the chocolate you wanted, would you want to be refused? Of course not. Yet, if you are to follow the Golden Rule of doing unto others what you would want returned in kind, shouldn't you give the child what he wants? Or consider the prisoner who is brought before the judge. Putting yourself in his place, you must know that you would want to be pardoned and set free, so why not free the fellow? Because there is a higher law than even the rule we call "golden."

I could give a dozen illustrations, and so could you, that would enlarge the question, Is the Golden Rule really Christian?—which is to say, is the Golden Rule always the most loving thing to do? Perhaps a more careful interpolation of the rule should be, "Do unto others whatever you *ought* to wish that others would do unto you." Without this, the rule could cover trading between drug dealers.

But if you do rewrite the rule that way, it becomes more complicated. How do you know for sure what really ought and ought not to be done for another? I hear faint echos of "Someday you'll thank me," or even, "Believe me, this hurts me worse than it does you." There is a certain arrogance in assuming what "ought" to be done for another. It was George Bernard Shaw who said, "Don't do unto others what you would have them do unto you; their tastes may be different." And we've all heard about the boy scout who helped three little old ladies across the street, two of whom didn't want to go.

What, in each situation, is the loving, caring thing to do for another? Figuring that out is a hard trick, but that is precisely the Christian trick. That's the whole shape of Christian ethics. Simply doing unto others what you would like them to do unto you may be little more than a crass expression of an acute unawareness of your own needs.

What it comes down to is that the Golden Rule could be little more than an expression of the "pain and pleasure principle"—to do to others the things that bring you pleasure, and refrain from doing unto others the things that bring you pain, whereas what is really called for in our relationships is a much deeper, more perceptive, more sensitive kind of love. A starting point for this kind of love, for example, is giving our excess produce to community food banks to be distributed to those in need. But if we are really concerned about hunger, love requires that we become better informed on why the problems of hunger exist and what systemic changes have to be made in our society to eliminate those problems. Meeting human needs at their deepest level takes time. It takes thinking. It takes slowing down, to love properly.

Edwin McNeill Poteat wrote this poem:

I know the road to Jericho, it's in a part of town
That's full of factories and filth. I've seen the folk go
    down,
Small folks, with roses in their cheeks and starlight in their
    eyes,
I've seen them fall among the thieves and heard their
    helpless cries.
When toiling took their roses red, and robbed them of
    their stars,

And left them pale and almost dead. The while, in
  motorcars,
The priests and Levites speeding by read of the latest
  crimes
In headlines spread in black or red across the evening
  Times.
It's hard for those in limousines to heal the hurt of man;
It was a slow-paced ass that bore that Good Samaritan.[1]

A lot of the time, we move too fast to see and to sense
the pain around us as love requires that we do. We may
give a little pleasure along the way, and avoid giving pain,
just as the Golden Rule says, and that becomes a
substitute for taking the time to look more deeply into the
world, or into one another's eyes, which is where the real
need is.

The prophet Jeremiah spoke in behalf of God: "Thus
says the Lord: Do justice and righteousness, and deliver
from the hand of the oppressor him who has been robbed.
And do no wrong or violence to the alien, the fatherless,
and the widow, nor shed innocent blood in this place"
(Jeremiah 22:3). Centuries before Jesus, the Jews were
realizing that high religion had something to do with
justice, righteousness, and caring. Judaism made this a
matter of law.

But the Christian religion is not a religion of law, and
the Golden Rule is not Christian, because no rule is
Christian. The Christian faith isn't a rule religion. It is a
religion of the Word made flesh; *Rules* made flesh. The
Christian faith is hammered out on the anvil of one's daily
life; it comes out in the form of one's love and liveliness,
and not of rules at all. It isn't even the same as
"principle," really, and the word "lifestyle" falls pretty
short.

That's one reason the heart of Christian faith is not
described by words as much as by symbols. For the
Christian community, the symbol is the cross, an enigma

which perhaps mystifies as much as it illumines. In one aspect, it is a mighty absurd symbol: Imagine, if you will, a society whose central symbol and identifying mark is a gas chamber or an electric chair. Then you have some idea of what Paul meant when he spoke of the cross as being a "stumbling block to Jews and folly to Gentiles" (1 Cor. 1:23).

For the cross in Jesus' time was an instrument of the death penalty, and our Master was executed like a common crook. Today we wear crosses on our lapels, around our necks, even in our ears, and the crosses on our altars are usually of shiny brass or polished mahogany. This may be all right, as long as we remember that the first cross was not worn but borne, and it was not a thing of beauty but a thing of ugliness and shame.

And so, can you imagine the folly in suggesting that the cross ought to be lifted up as a banner of victory, or knelt before as a symbol of power, or cherished as an expression of infinite love? Yet look at it now: The one symbol, whatever its form, which is common to all Christians the world over is the cross. It is not an arbitrary symbol. The fact that the cross was the Roman instrument of a most shameful death is not incidental; it is intentional. It has to do with the fact that a person in history, whose love for those who deserved it least was undeniable, and who met their betrayal not with a curse but with a prayer of forgiveness, came to be seen by the eyes of faith as a sort of lens through which we could see God's love for us all. "Behold, what manner of love is this?" we ask, bewildered.

A prison warden has reported that almost invariably, the last person to give up on a convict is his mother. That's how a good parent's heart works. And to redeem that lost child, said Frank Cairns, a heart would have to break. God's heart, too, said Cairns, has been broken by us. This is hard to bear; we grow ashamed and long to change—and at that point change begins to occur. That special, unqualified, no-strings-attached love does not just accept us; it makes us new. It not only receives who we are, it enables us to become who we're meant to be.

That kind of affirmation of love has long since left the Golden Rule in the dust. The Golden Rule has to do with how we should behave, but the Christian gospel is not first of all a message of how we should behave. It's a message about God's response to our misbehavior—a response that affirms us, accepts us, believes in us in spite of our behavior.

The Golden Rule by itself is not only unchristian, it's impossible. In a cartoon a questioner at a public meeting asks the speaker, "but just how are we going to have this brave new world with the same old people in it?"

That's the point. The Golden Rule does not make the same old people new—but the cross can. The cross, with its forceful reminder of a love that embraces us—all of us—including everything about us that is unembraceable, says, "You are loved just the way you are." That is what turns us inside out and makes us new. It's because of Jesus Christ that I know this, and that is why I am a Christian.

If the Golden Rule were to be Christian, it would have to be rewritten to read:

"Do unto others as God has already done unto you."

FOUR

Why Do the Good Suffer?

Scripture: Job 1:1, 13-22;
John 9:1-12

WHY DO the good suffer? This is a question with which we have all struggled. Elton Trueblood called it "the most persistent and the most difficult question the human mind knows." Why do the good and the innocent suffer so often when they don't deserve it, while on the other hand, we see scoundrels get away with crimes without punishment? It just isn't fair. If God is the God the Bible discloses, a God of justice and love, why does God let it happen? It looks like a clear-cut case of mismanagement.

The entire book of Job was written about this question, and Jesus also dealt with the problem. Quite frankly, most of the answers we've gotten elsewhere haven't been very satisfying. Sometimes we are told that what is lost in this life will be made up in heaven. Sometimes we've been told that it just looks as though the evil prosper, that if we really knew their lives from the inside, we'd know how they suffer, too.

But those answers leave something to be desired. What is desired is a frank and direct answer to the baffling question: Why does life seem to punish some people who, like Job, are "blameless and upright, who fear God, and turn away from evil"? I say it raises some questions, not only about life, but about God. No wonder Francis McConnell called this question "the parent of all serious skepticism."

In Jesus' time, there was an assumption that if someone was born with a disability, like blindness, it must be some sort of punishment or retribution for evil. That's why the disciples asked the question they did: "Who sinned, this man or his parents, that he was born blind?" (John 9:2). Jesus' answer was forthright. "Neither," he said, putting to rest the notion that disability resulted from a capricious or punitive God. That's not the way God works.

But then he goes on to say that the man was born blind "that the works of God might be made manifest in him." Now, that's a little troubling. At first glance, it looks as though God blinded the man in order that he could demonstrate something, make a case or prove a point, which would mean that God doesn't *love* people so much as God just *uses* people.

Well, it would be awfully hard to square that with everything else Jesus revealed about God, and that is what we would have to do to make that interpretation stick. The way to read the Bible, and that includes everything attributed to the mouth of Jesus, is to weigh every single verse of Scripture against everything Jesus said and did. And everything else Jesus said and did does not give us a picture of a God who uses people rather than loves them.

Let me say it more accurately: If God uses us, it is not in the way of malicious manipulation. God uses whatever we put at God's disposal; God can use whatever experience comes our way.

That's much different than saying God causes everything that happens to us. I don't believe that is true at all. I know there have been some who prefer to believe that God ordains everything that happens. That's in an effort to affirm that God is really sovereign of the universe, that God is in final control. But the notion that everything that happens is ordained by God is precisely what traps us in the dilemma. We begin to ask, If God is all powerful and all loving, how does one explain the suffering of the innocent? We conclude that either God is not as powerful as we think; or, being all powerful, God does not *care* as much as we think. Otherwise, God wouldn't permit unjust suffering.

But that overlooks an important third ingredient, in addition to the power and the love of God. Not only is God all powerful and all loving, but God loves us enough to choose to grant the human creature a large measure of freedom, freedom to reject the will of God, freedom to cheat, maim, and kill one another, freedom to inflict suffering on good and innocent people.

In other words, God could have created a different kind of universe, but God did not. God could have chosen to create a world in which history was the working out of a regular, daily formula; in which good people were rewarded and evil people were punished; in which the ledger was balanced at the end of every day or every week, or at least every month. But if God were to create a world like that, it would mean that God would have to govern our actions more directly and determine all events by divine manipulation.

Hence, instead of creating a law of gravity which was consistent, and upon which we could depend with certainty, God could interfere with that law whenever it threatened to hurt someone. When a baby fell out of a crib or a second-story window, or a plane ran out of fuel, or a mountain-climber lost her footing, God would intervene—provided those were all good and innocent people. God could allow a bullet to kill an evil person, but would stop a bullet to save a good life, or turn the wheel of a car so that only the drunk driver was killed, or halt a thief or rapist in his tracks.

That might sound like an improvement on creation, until you think about it a little. If God took that much direct action in the events of the world, which God would

33

have to do if the innocent were to be protected and the evil punished, it could only be at the expense of our freedom, and what point would there be left to life? It would be like a play that was already written and that no one was watching. It would be like playing a game in which the final score was already announced. I wouldn't want it that way and neither would you, and God knew that. So God chose not to limit his love, but to love us enough to limit the powers he could impose. God gave us freedom. There was great risk in that choice, very much like the risk parents take when they begin to set their children free, not knowing whether they are quite ready, having to stand by sometimes and watch them make foolish choices.

How it must hurt God to see us misuse our freedom, violate one another, and reject his will. I wonder sometimes if God ever regrets having made that choice of giving the human creature a radical degree of freedom that no other creature has. Apparently, God still believes it is a good tradeoff, and so do I. I'm glad God made the world the way it is, for most of what I have and enjoy and benefit from are the things I have not earned or created myself, but have inherited from the good efforts of others. Of course, that also means we suffer from the wrongs of others. Some people starve because others don't care. Some people are crippled because others drive carelessly. Some people die needlessly of illnesses for which we have not yet found cures because we've chosen to invest our wealth in missiles rather than medical research. All this happens because God chose to create a world in which we are affected by and depend upon each other. But I'm still glad God made the world as it is.

God could have waited to create humankind until the earth's creation were nearer to being finished, so that humans would not have set foot on earth until after the last volcano or earthquake or tidal wave had vanished.

But God brought us in before creation was done, to share in understanding and living with what some call "natural disasters," what insurance companies are fond of calling "acts of God."

So one answer to the question, Why do the good suffer? is simply that any guarantees that the good would not suffer involve alternatives in creation that we would not want.

It is correct, then, to say that God does permit suffering. But that is a vastly different thing from saying that God inflicts suffering, for it is not in God's heart to do so, even upon the evil. God's love extends to both the well-behaved and the misbehaved people alike.

That's when we feel the injustice the most—when we discover that God loves the members of the Mafia no less than the members of a monastic order. We have, of course, some pretty firm judgments about that, but they are our own, not God's. Augustine told of a vision he once had of standing before God with a bitter enemy and saying, "God, why don't you destroy this wicked person?" and hearing God reply, "Which one?"

It is, in fact, most fortunate for all of us that God's love doesn't diminish at every point where we disappoint him. We cannot have it both ways. If God is to love us without condition, God must love everyone without condition. Suffering is a part of life, and it is not doled out according to the deserts of the individual any more than is God's love.

Given this fact, there is still more to be said. You and I have a lot of power and freedom to reduce human suffering in the world. For example, medical research has reduced suffering and eradicated many illnesses in our society. As a diabetic, I simply would not be alive if someone had not developed a way to inject insulin. My doctors tell me they will probably have a perfect solution to diabetes within ten years. One of the greatest causes of suffering in our time is cancer. I have no doubt that the day will come when even that will have a cure, and whether that day comes soon or later will depend in part on how much talent and money we devote to research. Ironic, isn't it, that our military defense is taken from our taxes, while cancer research is funded by voluntary donations. Jesus might even say, "The nation that seeks to save its life with more nuclear warheads will lose it to cancer." We are not powerless to make decisions about such choices. There are, of course, governments everywhere that are guilty of atrocities against people. I cannot do much about those. What hurts most is the knowledge that *our* government is participating in atrocities against innocent people, and we *can* do something about that.

So one uncomfortable answer to the question, Why do the good and innocent suffer? is that we don't do more to reduce the suffering. It also needs to be said that not only does God permit suffering, and grant us the freedom to respond to it as we will, but sometimes God may even refuse to alleviate it. Thornton Wilder wrote a short play about a crippled doctor who stood beside the pool of Bethesda, waiting for the waters to be troubled that he might be healed. (That legend is recorded in the fifth chapter of John.) But the angel who troubled the waters said to this ailing doctor who had not been able to heal himself:

> Stand back. Healing is not for you. Without your wound, where would your power be, that sends your low voice trembling into the hearts of men? We ourselves, the very angels of God in heaven, cannot persuade the wretched and blundering children of earth as can one human being broken on the wheels of living. In love's service, only the wounded soldiers will do.

Sometimes those who suffer are helped most by those who have suffered. That's what "support groups" are all about—people with similar pains who can support one another more effectively than can people who do not know those pains firsthand. A most dramatic example and a primary model of a support group is Alcoholics Anonymous. People recovering from alcoholism, from which they can never be cured, can be of more help to other alcoholics than can nonalcoholics; their capacity to help in the healing process is not *in spite* of their disease but precisely *because* of it.

Perhaps you are familiar with the words of the poet Francis Thompson, who was also an alcoholic. He wrote in "The Hound of Heaven" about his own experience, which begins with the words,

> I fled Him, down the nights and down the days;
> I fled Him down the arches of the years;
> I fled Him down the labyrinthine ways
> Of my own mind; and in the mist of tears
> I hid from Him, and under running laughter.

Later in the poem, he quotes God as saying:

> All which I took from thee I did but take,
> Not for thy harms,
> But just that thou might'st seek it in My arms.
> All which thy child's mistake
> Fancies as lost, I have stored for thee at home:
> Rise, clasp My hand, and come![1]

Suffering need not be an obstacle in our path to God, but it can be an avenue to God. It is not simply a necessary evil that comes with the good; it actually bears positive attributes of its own. Hence Paul goes so far as to say, "I rejoice in my sufferings" (Col. 1:24). This leads to a question that is much more important than the one with which we began. The final question is not, *Why* do the good suffer? but, *How* do the good suffer?—though we must

37

keep in mind that to count ourselves among the "good" is to be a bit presumptuous.

We can suffer in self-pity, we can suffer in bitterness, we can suffer in martyrdom, we can even suffer to punish ourselves. Or, we can suffer in the same way that we live the rest of our lives: as an offering to God. Not only may we endure suffering, we may use it. Suffering may come in a way that we didn't elect, but we may elect what to do with it. This is the meaning of the second part of Jesus' answer to the disciples' question regarding the blind man: "He was born blind . . . that the works of God might be made manifest in him" (John 9:3). They don't have to be, but they can be, if we choose to let God be manifested in us.

Someone once said to a person who was suffering, "Suffering does color life, doesn't it?" "Yes," came the reply. "And I intend to choose the color." If there is anyone who has reason to understand that answer, it is the Christian who worships and lives before the image of the cross.

FIVE

Things I Wish Jesus Hadn't Said

Scripture: Matthew 10:34-39

I F IT were up to me, I'd eliminate a lot of pages from the New Testament, and that would include a lot of paragraphs out of the mouth of Jesus.

Oh, I wouldn't touch those things we like to hear—comforting words such as "Him who comes to me I will not cast out," or "Neither do I condemn you; go, and do not sin again." I wouldn't tamper with assuring words such as, "Fear not, little flock, for it is your Father's good pleasure to give you the kingdom." I'd leave intact that refreshing invitation, "Come to me, all who labor and are heavy laden, and I will give you rest," and that reminder that I am worth more than many sparrows. What a feast for the hungry heart those words are; what a tonic for an anxious soul. What a sense of security so many have come to feel in this world as a result of receiving this message of a God who loves us beyond our understanding and strengthens us in time of need. I'm glad Jesus said all those things, and I believe them.

It's those other things that I would just as soon he hadn't said at all, precisely because there appears to be no joy in them. They sound harsh, almost cruel; and on first glance, they seem wholly out of keeping with almost everything else he said.

One thing I'd like to red-pencil is that reference in scripture in which Jesus says, "Do not think that I have come to bring peace on earth; I have not come to bring peace, but a sword" (Matt. 10:34). That can't help confusing us. We recall elsewhere his blessing the peacemakers. He instructed us, "All who take the sword will perish by the sword" (Matt. 26:52). Yet here he is quoted as saying, "I have not come to bring peace, but a sword." How I wish he hadn't said that!

Of course, we all have our bad days, and maybe this was one of his. But I don't think it is that easy. For one thing, we do remember that Jesus often used words as a poet uses them. This is a problem a lot of us have in understanding the Bible: knowing when the words are to be taken literally and when they are to be understood poetically or metaphorically. When Jesus said, "I came to bring a sword," we don't expect to see him swinging a weapon any more than when he says, "I am the door," we expect to see him swinging on hinges. He was speaking metaphorically—poetically.

It seems trivial to make the point, but you would be surprised how often in the course of history, from the Crusades even up to the present day, wars have been justified by just such a simple-minded reading of scripture. Many other kinds of mischief have been perpetrated as well by Christians who have insisted on taking every phrase of the Bible *literally* instead of *seriously*.

I take what he said seriously, which is exactly why I wish he hadn't said those words. For in using this figure of speech, Jesus reminds me that much as I might wish it so, the Christian faith does not stop with peace of mind and a rosy outlook on life. It is not all contentment and bliss. There is often great discontent as well; there is tension, there is conflict. These, too, are results of Christian commitment, and this is what I wish Jesus had not said, because the Christian faith and the Christian life could be so simple if it were just a matter of peace. But he said it in no uncertain terms: "I have come to set a man against his father, and a daughter against her mother, and a daughter-in-law against her mother-in-law; and a man's foes will be those of his own household" (Matt. 10:35).

In other words, follow Jesus and there will be conflict, even among those who are closest to one another. And this is not, in fact, a contradiction of what Jesus says elsewhere about joy and blessedness. He's rounding out his full statement to tell us, "There is no gain without pain," that the hardship often reveals the meaning, that tears often make the rainbow. He's not saying that conflict is the last word any more than crucifixion is, but that it is an unavoidable word, just as crucifixion is. Thank goodness Jesus didn't come just to bring tranquility. What a bore.

I think of marriage and the people I know who are frightened to death of conflict in marriage and avoid it at all costs. That's simply not being realistic. Of course, unnecessary conflict in marriage can be minimized. A soldier on the battlefront kept getting nagging letters from his wife, to which he finally responded, "Will you please quit bugging me and let me fight this war in peace!"

But someone has wisely said that the notion of two people living intimately together for twenty-five years without a cross word between them reflects a quality to be admired only in sheep. Intimacy inevitably means conflict from time to time, and when life's most basic and intimate questions are introduced, questions of faith and ultimate commitment, as Jesus was doing, conflict between friends, family, and lovers is virtually unavoidable.

Jesus' personal experience figures here, I suspect. We have evidence that on at least one occasion, his own family came to take him home because they thought he was "beside himself." No doubt he knew what "division" meant—enstrangement from those closest to you. And although Jesus' first followers were Jews, he was really calling them out of and away from the limits of orthodox

41

Judaism. Nothing could possibly generate more conflict within a family than that. When a good Jew turned his back on his family religion to commit his life to this alleged Son of God, it was worse than for this family member to have died, as far as the family was concerned. In fact, in certain Oriental religions today, when one leaves the faith to become a Christian, the family publicly carries a casket through the streets to symbolize the convert's death. It's as if Jesus had come to bring a sword.

I also wish Jesus hadn't said, "He who loves father or mother more than me is not worthy of me" (Matt. 10:37). It sounds as though Jesus is saying, "Choose between your family and God." He is not really. But he *is* saying, as he frequently said, that one must choose where one's ultimate commitment lies. In all of our dearest human relationships, we may love each other, but we do not own each other. Only God owns us. Therefore, we acknowledge that our first obligation of devotion is to God. Is this bad? Is it disappointing? Not when I reflect on it. Actually, it is wonderful, for it is one of the surest guarantees I have of the eternity of my relationships with those who mean most to me.

There is no one on earth I love more than I love my wife and my three children. Yet I believe that my ultimate commitment is to God, and that as I live out that commitment faithfully, I shall be the more faithful husband and father. Where I have been faithless in my family roles, I have been out of touch with God. It is God who lends meaning to all my roles—husband, father, grandfather, pastor, citizen, friend. My love for God takes nothing away from my love for others; it can only add to it. And just as God has made possible the relationships I have that mean the most to me, so these relationships are secure in God throughout this life and beyond. I need to love God more than anyone or anything else in order that I can love my family and everyone else better than I do. I guess Jesus had to say those words, didn't he?

And he had to say those other words about taking up a cross daily and following him. I could have done without that. I mean, following him is all right, but taking up a cross—daily? I much prefer those other words: "Take my yoke upon you, and learn from me. . . For my yoke is easy, and my burden is light" (Matt. 11:29-30). If it were up to me, I'd settle for words like that, and edit out all those references to having to bear a cross. I'd much prefer to come to church just to get away from the pains and problems of the world rather than be reminded of them. I'd rather love the people I enjoy loving, rather than having to stretch the circle of my concern to people I don't much like. I'd rather be content with what I know and what I believe than expose myself to new truth and new experience that might force me to change in some ways.

W. C. Fields was once caught by a friend as he was reading the Bible. His friend asked, "What are you doing?" and Fields replied, "Looking for loopholes."

I'd sure like to find an easier way into discipleship if I could, but every time I try, I run smack up against the Master saying, "He who does not take his cross and follow me is not worthy of me" (Matt. 10:38).

Have you seen those bumper stickers that say, "Honk if you love Jesus"? Well, I saw one once that said, "If you love Jesus, tithe. Anybody can honk." That says it all for me. It's one thing, and a fairly simple thing, to praise the name of Jesus, but to take his word and his lifestyle into society, that is the hard part. Any group can get together and study the Bible or pray or design worship services and preach and sing. That is the easy part. But where are we spilling the blood of our lives for the lonely and the hungry and the walking wounded, whether down the street or around the world? That's what is hard, but that is where the measure is taken.

If Jesus were preaching to us today, he would not only be saying some things we wish he wouldn't say, he'd be asking some questions we would not want to answer. For instance: "How much money are you giving away these days in comparison with what you are keeping for yourself and your loved ones?" Or: "How hard are you working at learning new truth and at understanding your faith?" He might even ask, "Is there a single human issue in the world to which you are relating yourself in some creative way in order to draw the world a hair's breadth closer to God's dream for it?"

And if we turned Jesus off at those points of his message, we'd be evading the one thing that might make the difference between life as a drag and life as a joy: this invitation to bear a cross is not really in contrast to those gentler words about an easy yoke. They are part of the same truth.

Let me explain what I mean by calling attention to the fact that there is no work so hard as work without purpose. The torture of the prisoner who makes little rocks out of big rocks is not just the physical energy he exerts, but the purposelessness of it all. I've known people whose routine jobs were drab and uninspiring because all the job did for them was to make possible a paycheck. Then when the person got married the job took on new life, because it suddenly became the means of supporting a spouse and family. However, even this is seldom enough. Ultimately, a person must look for a job in terms of what it does for society: does it add or detract, does it help or hinder? If a person sells paint or pants or pennynails, that person can have the feeling of providing goods that make a difference to the comfort or well-being of people. If a person delivers mail or picks up trash or fixes hair or sells insurance, that person can feel the joys of performing human service. A work that does not provide that satisfaction is twice as hard at half the effort.

John Nelson gave us all the advice we need on this point. He said, "God doesn't call any man or woman to a trivial or unimportant life work. If you can't see your job as being somehow vital and meaningful to humankind, change it or get out of it."

One time, when I asked a woman to take a job in my church, I made the mistake of saying, "The job won't really be that hard." Her reply to my remark was, "If the job isn't hard, I don't want it." She was simply saying that a difficult task is easier than a simple task because it means more.

So here is Jesus, saying, "Lest you expect Christian discipleship to be a snap, let me warn you that it is not. It will cost you, you can be sure of that; and you can also be sure that if it didn't cost you anything, neither would it give you anything." As I catch myself sometimes wishing that Christian discipleship didn't cost quite so much, I don't have to look very far to see that the cost I'm paying isn't nearly what some Christians are paying in this world. And I also remember that I get value received for every cost I pay, and when I refuse to assume the cost, I cheat myself and I cheat God. Consequently, Jesus' words, "Take up your cross" are *part* of the truth, "I am the life." You cannot have one without the other. All of which is summed up in his statement, "He who loses his life for my sake will find it" (Matt. 10:39).

Sometimes I wish Jesus hadn't said these things; but you understand, don't you? Have you ever, on occasion, wished you didn't have to go to work? Have you ever, on occasion, wished there weren't such creatures as children? Then you know how it is that we sometimes wish out of existence the very things that give our lives their greatest satisfaction and joy.

So when I wish Jesus had left these things unsaid, I need only remember how bare my life would be if he had not said them and, moreover, had not lived them.

45

SIX

Things in the Bible Jesus Didn't Believe

Scripture: Jeremiah 31:31-34;
Matthew 5:17-20

THERE IS one thing that you and I have that Jesus never had, and that is a New Testament. Jesus had a bible, of course, the scriptures of the Jews. It was mainly what Christians refer to as the Old Testament. But the New Testament was produced after Jesus' death and resurrection.

So when I write about "things in the Bible Jesus didn't believe," I'm talking about the Old Testament. I know that "biblical game-playing" is an easy means of justifying our assertions. But there really are things in the Old Testament that Jesus didn't believe, and he said so. The reason I think that point is worth a sermon is that there are many Christians who still believe things that Jesus didn't believe. And I think to believe them is not to believe Jesus.

Let's look at some familiar incidents which may illustrate what I mean. Take this one in John 8:3-5:

> The scribes and the Pharisees brought a woman who had been caught in adultery, and placing her in the midst they said to him, "Teacher, this woman has been caught in the act of adultery. Now in the law Moses commanded us to stone such. What do you say about her?"

The scenario is clear. They had already heard enough of Jesus to suspect that when push came to shove, he would probably recommend something other than stoning the woman, and they wanted to trap him in public. The law was the law. Leviticus 20:10 reads, "If a man commits adultery with the wife of his neighbor, both the adulterer and the adulteress shall be put to death." That's in your Bible. Check it.

Do you believe that that is God's will? Jesus didn't. Of course, he didn't say that. Instead, he went with it and went well beyond it. He said, after a prolonged silence, you recall, "Let him who is without sin among you be the first to throw a stone at her" (John 8:7). No stones were thrown. Jesus' words had the intended effect. They enabled the crowd to see that the law, as written in the Torah, was not enough. It's not so much that it was wrong, in suggesting that we should be held accountable when we hurt or violate one another, but that it's altogether too easy to draw simple lines between the guilty and the innocent, and that ultimately, we all stand under judgment.

The law was incomplete as an expression of God's will. Jesus revealed a fuller expression of that will. God's will is that we go far beyond the dictums of the law, with a righteousness that exceeds all of that. Hence, Jesus *fulfilled* the law.

Or Jesus might have said, "Turn in your Bibles to Deuteronomy 24:1, and read where it says, 'When a man takes a wife and marries her, if then she finds no favor in his eyes because he has found some indecency in her . . . he writes her a bill of divorce and puts it in her hand and sends her out of his house . . .' " Just as easy as that! It's in your Bibles. I think however Jesus might have said, "I don't believe in that." He did say, "I say to you that every one who divorces his wife, except on the grounds of unchastity, makes her an adulteress" (Matt. 5:31-32). Now, Jesus was not substituting one hard and fast rule for another hard and fast practice. He was going beyond the vision of the law and saying, "Wives are not properly to be disposed of at whim like an old coat. The law does not convey clearly enough that God claims women as rightful children of God quite as much as God claims men as rightful children of God."

Jesus didn't just say that the law was not enough; he showed it—by keeping company with women, even speaking to strange women in the street, eating with publicans and sinners which no devout Jew would do, healing on the Sabbath day, which was forbidden by law—how many times was Jesus called into account for violating Jewish law? And each time, Jesus was saying, "I don't believe it. I don't believe *that* law is a careful expression of God's will. It doesn't even express the intent of God's law."

So Jesus didn't abolish law, he fulfilled it. He didn't terminate it, he went beyond it. But in doing so, he implied, "There are certain things in the Bible I don't believe."

He was pretty direct about it in the Sermon on the Mount: "You have heard that it was said, 'An eye for an eye and a tooth for a tooth.' " "It's in the Bible," Jesus might have said, "but I don't believe it." "I say to you, Do not resist one who is evil. But if any one strikes you on the right cheek, turn to him the other also; and if any one would sue you and take your coat, let him have your cloak as well; and if any one forces you to go one mile, go with him two miles" (Matt. 5:38-41).

You see, we are really faced with a choice here. Here are two quite different directives for moral behavior: the law of "an eye for an eye" and the Sermon on the Mount. Both of them are biblical, but only one of them is Christian. The person who elects to follow Jesus will find himself saying, as Jesus did, "There are some things in the Bible I don't believe. I do not believe God's will is that we simply return kind for kind when we are harmfully treated. God's will is that we be not only more compassionate, but more creative than that."

Now again, if you simply take Jesus' metaphor literally and expose your vulnerability every time someone attacks you personally or nationally, you will end up being everyone's doormat. That is not what Jesus means. What he means is that if your primary concern is to defend your superiority and come out ahead, the inevitable result is two human adversaries beating and scarring each other until one or both give up, or kill one another.

On the other hand, if you want to move, as Jesus does, beyond hostility to creativity where everyone benefits, you turn your attention to what makes the other angry, what has hurt the other, and what solution might bring power to both parties. That's a philosophy and strategy that we may not want to buy at all. I'm not saying it's easy. I'm not saying it's popular, and I'm certainly not saying it's uncostly. I'm only saying it's what Jesus was talking about.

But it's not what the Bible says at every point. The Old Testament is replete with references to a vengeful God punishing with violence. That, says the Old Testament at many points, is the kind of God that God is. I hear Jesus saying, "I don't believe it. I know people used to believe it about God, and I know there is an excitement and satisfaction in the thought that God will strew the bodies of our enemies across the field. But I don't believe that is the kind of God that God is. Nor is it the kind of person God calls you to be."

When people want to support toughness instead of strength, or retaliation instead of reconciliation, or prejudice instead of tolerance, they often go to the Bible for support, and they often find it, but not in Jesus.

"Tit for tat" is a very simple way to think about the world. Remember when Jesus and his disciples saw a blind man, and his disciples asked him, "Rabbi, who sinned, this man or his parents, that he was born blind?" It was standard understanding in that day that God punishes the evil and rewards the good. Jesus didn't answer their question; he said, "It was not that this man sinned, or his parents, but that the works of God might be made manifest in him" (John 9:2-3).

Remember, Jesus got into trouble with the scribes and Pharisees because he didn't believe or practice all of the conventional laws of Judaism. He didn't reject the law outright, he rejected it as the final word. Hence, he extended or fulfilled the law by revealing a fuller word—and that's why we are called Christians. Because we believe Jesus discloses the latest word about who God is, what God does, and what God expects.

This is an important point: Judaism, as expressed in the Old Testament, is a religion of law. Although there are moments of God's grace to be found in the Old Testament, the heart of the Hebrew faith is law, because it is a precious ingredient of the covenant between God and the people of Israel. If the Israelites obey the law, God will bring them to a land of milk and honey. The ultimate characteristic of the Old Testament God is insistence upon the law. And this is where Jesus departs. Jesus believed that people were not made for the law, but laws were made for people. Not that the law was unimportant; but it was not enough. If our focus is on the law, we will miss the point. If our focus is on the spirit of the law—the intention—we begin to come closer.

First of all, Jesus took two commandments out of the law, one from Exodus and one from Leviticus, and said (Luke 10:27), "Love the Lord your God with all your heart, and with all your soul, and with all your strength, and with all your mind; and your neighbor as yourself." He based his entire life and teaching on this foundation.

These are a pair of laws you cannot hammer out into particular legal prescriptions. When Jesus used the word "law," he used it much the way it is used in speaking of the twelve Boy Scout laws. Scouts are called to be trustworthy, loyal, helpful, friendly, courteous, kind, obedient, cheerful, thrifty, brave, clean, and reverent. These, like Jesus' two commandments, are requirements to live by, not ordinances to obey. The spirit of the law fulfills the letter of the law and therefore is much more important.

There must have been many things in the old Bible that Jesus didn't believe. Where the law excluded women and children, Jesus included women and a set a child in their midst as a model. Where the law judged publicans and sinners, Jesus ate dinner with them. Where the law looked down on non-Jews, Jesus told a story in which the hero was a Samaritan. Jesus did not believe in racial or sexual discrimination, or economic oppression, or arrogant nationalism, even if they were supported by the old Bible. Is it any wonder they put him away?

And when they did put him away, that's when he departed most radically from the old Bible and its laws. Those who did believe that Jesus was the long-awaited Messiah, and some did, believed what the old Bible told them: that this Messiah would vindicate the Jews, vanquish their enemies, and make the Jews victorious over all other peoples. But Jesus didn't believe that about the Messiah, and in Gethsemane he redefined the role the Messiah—the Christ—was called to play. He went to the cross as the suffering servant envisioned only by the prophets of old.

Most incredible, the cross has become for us not a sign of punishment, but a symbol of forgiveness. Despite every reason God has to chastise us, reject us, punish us for our faithlessness, God meets us with the same love as if we had pleased him entirely. This does not let us off the hook, but moves us to love—to offer understanding to those who put us down, to forgive those who wrong us, to extend confidence to those who have no confidence in themselves, because that's how God continually meets us.

Ours, in other words, is not a religion of law, but a religion of grace.

If there are things in the Bible Jesus didn't believe, and I've tried to show that there are, it is only because God's love for us, and God's expectations of us, are far greater than the Bible often specifies. Jesus said the intent of the law is to be obeyed, and that calls us not to fall short of it, but to go far beyond it to achieve a potential that exceeds the "goodness" of even the scribes and the Pharisees. Our final guideline, therefore, is not the words of the Bible in general, but the spirit of Christ in particular, which reveals the will of God.

SEVEN

The Old Looking-up-in-the-air Trick

Scripture: Matthew 7:21-29

YOU'VE SEEN the trick, of course. The Smothers Brothers called it "the old looking-up-in-the-air trick," but they weren't the first to do it. Perhaps we have all seen it: one or two people stand around looking up in the air, and curious bystanders gather to join in looking up in the air to see what people are looking up in the air to see. Of course, there's nothing significant to see. The perpetrators sneak off chuckling as they look back at this crowd, all looking up in the air—at nothing. It's a great fooler.

The old looking-up-in-the-air trick has taken many forms in our recent history. Remember a decade or so ago, when it was predicted that on April 19 of that year, California was supposed to drop into the ocean? Some people sold their property—to people who didn't believe it, of course—and some folks at least arranged to be out of the state on April 19, just in case.

And a few years ago, astrologers and crystal-ball gazers had predicted that there would be a solar eclipse and realignment of the planets, which would result in the end of the world. In India, Hindu priests were surrounded by anxious people who feared the collision of the planets. And in Chicago, a citizen offered a soothsayer half of everything he owned if he would exercise his power to keep the universe from blowing up. Now there's a deal I wish someone had offered me. I'd have taken half his wealth and guaranteed him the universe wouldn't blow up; and if I were proven wrong, who's to know?

The problem, according to Norman Cousins, who wrote about this phenomenon, was that although humankind's abode on earth was in danger, most people were looking in the wrong place for the cause of the trouble. It wasn't the planets, but men, who were going crazy. People were looking into outer space for disorder, rather than into inner space.

The church, too, has played the looking-up-in-the-air trick from time to time. Sometimes it has stood around on street corners pointing up to the sky, diverting its followers' attention from this world to some other one—heaven. People were told that on earth they were but sojourners in a strange land, and that their task was to remain as patient and unspoiled, as untouched by this world, as possible, until arrival in their real home.

If you separate some words of Jesus from all else that he said and did and was, you can compose a picture of the Christian faith in which the action that really counts and the place that really matters is somewhere else, later on, not here and now. If that isn't looking up in the air, then I don't know what is.

You can get that straight from Jesus if you pick your verses right. "You always have the poor with you," he said, which sounds as if Jesus didn't care for the destitute. Or it was reported elsewhere that he said, "the poor have good news preached to them." Big deal!—having Good News preached to you when you've just lost your job and you are on your last denarius, with a hut full of hungry children. This is the picture you get of Jesus' concern for earthly, human problems only if you clip out and throw away all those other verses of his, about giving and caring and sharing, even with those who don't deserve a thing from you or will never pay you back.

In a day when it wouldn't have made any sense for Jesus to talk about government welfare programs, he talked quite a bit about individual responsibility for human problems in the world. Now that these problems are set in more complex social contexts, it is absurd to suggest that Jesus would discourage his disciples from becoming involved in every possible, legitimate way. The looking-up-in-the-air gag bypasses these human needs and says the poor will get their reward in the next life, if they behave.

There's another way in which the church has sometimes played the old waiting game. It has said nothing is required of humankind but patience, particularly patience with other people's problems! Again a misreading of scripture, or at least a misunderstanding of the background of scripture, can lead one to the conclusion that the most devout Christian is the one who waits in patience, who doesn't do something, but just stands there.

There are times when that *is* the right thing to do. Theologian H. Richard Niebuhr spoke of "the grace of doing nothing." There are times when it is appropriate to sing,

> Be still, my soul: the Lord is on thy side;
> Bear patiently the cross of grief or pain;
> Leave to thy God to order and provide.

There were chapters in biblical history in which the community of faith was so completely powerless, and matters looked so utterly futile, that the only choices were either to give up in despair or to wait in faith. It is in those times that the devout Christian is a faithful waiter. However, the present day is no such time. We are not powerless; matters are not futile. There are ways in which we can, indeed, give a hand to "the least of these." Yet we

55

still hear some churches and preachers admonishing us to stay clean from the contamination of reality, to have nothing to do with social and human issues, for they are not the concern of the church. We are told to purify ourselves in preparation for the imminent coming of the Lord, who will solve our problems for us and set things straight for the faithful.

Here's a poet who sounds very much like a rebel of a recent decade, one of those writers who were called "Angry Young Men." He addresses these words to an evangelist who is playing this "waiting game":

> You come along . . . tearing your shirt . . . yelling about
>   Jesus.
> Where do you get that stuff?
> What do you know about Jesus?
> You tell people living in shanties Jesus is going to fix it
> up all right with them by giving them mansions in the skies
> after they're dead and the worms have eaten them.
> You tell $6-a-week department store girls all they need is
>   Jesus;
> You take a steel trust wop, dead without having lived,
>   gray and
> shrunken at forty years of age, and you tell him to look at
> Jesus on the cross and he'll be all right.
> You tell poor people they don't need any more on pay day
>   and even
> if it's fierce to be out of a job, Jesus'll fix that up all right
> all they gotta do is take Jesus the way you say.
> I'm telling you Jesus wouldn't stand for the sort of stuff
> you're handing out. Jesus played it different. The bankers
> and lawyers of Jerusalem got their sluggers and mur-
>   derers to
> go after Jesus just because Jesus wouldn't play their game.
> Jesus didn't sit in with the big thieves . . . I don't want a
>   lot
> of gab from a bunkshooter in my religion . . .

I ask you to come through and show me where you're
  pouring out
the blood of your life . . . [1]

Those aren't the words of a poet of the Beat
Generation in the fifties, of a hippie of the sixties, or a
protestor of the seventies. The lines are from Carl
Sandburg, who predates most of us.

There's nothing new about the church playing the old
looking-up-in-the-air trick, and nothing new about
criticisms of it—beginning with Jesus himself. "Not every
one who says to me, 'Lord, Lord,' shall enter the kingdom
of heaven," Jesus said in Matthew 7:21. Mouthing all the
pious words in the hymnody will never be enough. "Every
one then who hears these words of mine and does them,"
he says, "will be like a wise man who built his house upon
the rock . . . And every one who hears these words of
mine and does not do them will be like a foolish man . . ."
(Matt. 7:24, 26).

Riding in the wake of that error is an opposite and
equally grievous error, and that is to believe, literally,
that God only helps those who help themselves. I'd call it
"the old nose-to-the-ground routine"; it assumes that
whatever is going to be done, we have to do, because it's a
cinch God isn't going to. It sounds as though what they
are really saying is, "Look, brother, don't depend on God
because all your power comes from inside you." And
that, I think, is wrong. There is help God gives us before
and after we help ourselves. The secret of the Christian
life seems to be to master that balance between going and
letting go, between doing and letting God do. It means
not acting as though *we* were in charge of history. But it
also means not waiting for God to dream up all the
answers, mobilize all the power, and solve all the
problems without us.

It means that the land of milk and honey perpetually promised will never come from just waiting and doing nothing. It will require planning; it will involve work, and perhaps some hard changes.

If you doubt the truth of all this, check Scripture. Read the first chapter of the book of Acts, beginning with the sixth verse:

So when they had come together, they asked him, "Lord, will you at this time restore the kingdom of Israel?" He said to them, "It is not for you to know times or seasons which the Father has fixed by his own authority. But you shall receive power when the Holy Spirit has come upon you; and you shall be my witnesses in Jerusalem and in all Judea and Samaria and to the end of the earth." And when he had said this, as they were looking on, he was lifted up, and a cloud took him out of their sight. And while they were gazing into heaven as he went, behold, two men stood by them in white robes, and said, "Men of Galilee, why do you stand looking into heaven? . . ."

EIGHT

The Cross and a Busted Valentine

Scripture: Hosea 3;
John 15:9-17

THE SUBJECT, as you may have guessed, is love: one word, four letters, and a thousand meanings. We are wiser than to think that the word always means the same whenever it is used. There are kinds of love that mean a feeling and other kinds that do not refer to feeling at all. There are kinds of love that bear responsibility and others that settle for kicks. A *Playboy* cartoon reveals a certain insight when it shows a thoroughly rumpled young man and an equally rumpled young woman in a passionate embrace as the boy says, "Why speak of love at a time like this?"

The object of love makes a difference, and there is a broad gap between meaning "I love you," and meaning, "I love *me,* therefore I want you."

Love is a complicated thing, often a very confusing thing, both to the giver and to the recipient. Not only that, but love is always a very risky thing. The first risk of any love extended is that it may not be returned, or that love once given may now be withheld. And that is painful, and the more severe perhaps because often it must be borne in silence, without even the loved one knowing. A broken heart is at least as painful as a broken leg, and usually slower in the healing. One who speaks of "puppy love" or "merely infatuation" is flippant and does not understand—that love on any level can turn sour and even cause one to wish that love were not a fact of life.

59

C. S. Lewis said, "To love at all is to be vulnerable. Love anything and your heart will certainly be wrung and possibly broken."

I remember the first time it ever sank into me that my love for a woman could have anything at all to do with my love for God. I had been taught that love of God and love of neighbor were inseparable. But somehow, I guess I had thought that love for a member of the opposite sex was different and somehow separate. But I learned that just because love may be romantic or even sexual does not mean that that love is somehow the opposite of my love for God. It can be one means by which I express my love for God.

By the same token, when my "valentine gets busted" and my heart broken, that is not unrelated to my relationship with God either. Any experience I can have, that somehow provides a window through which I can understand God more clearly, and understand my relationship with God more carefully, is an experience I do well to have, no matter how painful. The experience of a broken heart is one such experience. For one thing, it awakens me to the fact that I have more in common with Jesus than I thought I had; for Jesus, too, had a heart, and we are told that for all the physical torture and loss of blood he suffered at his crucifixion, he died of a broken heart.

His ministry, it seemed, had been characterized by a broken heart—the broken heart of a lover suffering the slings and arrows of unrequited love. Oh, not the love of a man rejected by a woman, though I don't for a moment doubt the possibility that Jesus knew what it was to fall in love with a woman and know that it wasn't for him, which may have been a deep and secret pain of his life. But I'm speaking of the love of a man for humanity, in which we see the love of God for the world. After many months of self-giving ministry and careful explanation, Jesus hears one of his closest disciples say, "Lord, show us the Father." Brokenhearted, Jesus could only respond, "Have I been with you so long, and yet you do not know me, Philip?" (John 14:8, 9).

This was a lover who sat on a hillside overlooking a city saying, "O Jerusalem, Jerusalem, how often would I have held you and loved you, but you would not . . ." Society's ultimate rejection of the love of God, as seen in the crucifixion, is a metaphor for the lack of love that God encounters still. He or she who has known what it is to have love rejected or not responded to, knows something of the brokenheartedness of God, who calls us and does not hear us answer.

The Old Testament prophets were highly creative in their proclamation of what they believed to be God's word to humankind, and Hosea was one of the most creative. It came to him that God called him to marry a deliberately promiscuous woman. So he sought Gomer, a harlot, an adulteress, and he had children by her and called her to be faithful to him only, but she was not. Hosea's experience of marrying and being faithful to a faithless woman, illustrated to him the agony of God in loving a faithless people.

The Bible makes great use of the image of the prostitute and the act of adultery as indicative of the behavior of a faithless Israel, or a faithless person. And yet God, despite our behavior, continues to be faithful to us!

How thin and pale our love appears next to that of God; how full of talk, but short of action; all smoke but no fire. It reminds me of the lad who sent his beloved a valentine telegram. Not being too creative, he wrote on the form and handed it to the telegrapher: "I love you, I love you, I love you." "That's only nine words," said the agent. "You can get ten for the same price." So the lad thought some more, taxing his creativity to the limit, and decided

61

on a final message which read, "I love you, I love you, I love you. Regards."

To be sure, the *eros* of the valentine is not to be confused with the *agape* of the cross. But while the two are different, they are not unrelated. And just possibly the "busted valentine" could open the way to an insight concerning the meaning of the cross—not only in the way of understanding God's pain, but of knowing what to do with our own.

For what do you do when your love is rejected and you are left helpless and alone, when behind your facade of cheerfulness is a heart broken in a dozen places? What do you say when occasionally a tear slips out? In the words of a song of my youth, "It's my funny way of laughing"; or in the words of a song of my parents' youth, "Smoke gets in your eyes."

What do you do?

First of all, I suppose you do what Jesus did and express the forsakenness you feel—to someone and to God. And having been thus honest with life, you may then proceed to do what Jesus also did, and yield up the whole affair to God and ask him to make of it what he will.

George Bernard Shaw wrote that Jesus was executed upon a thick stick of wood, but he always had a way of getting hold of the right end of it. How do you get hold of the right end of a broken love? How do you *see* a cross or *put* a cross in the midst of a broken heart? I think there are ways, and again it is Jesus who gives us the clues. Jesus could have just wallowed in his misery and felt sorry for himself. Instead, he cooperated with God in making the very experience of pain itself a further vehicle for demonstrating God's love.

So it is with that scene of the crucifixion. I cannot describe the power for me in Jesus' prayer for my forgiveness at the moment when he had every reason to curse me. You see, the response a person makes to a rejecting lover is really a measure of the depth of one's love. If that response is anger and a desire to hurt back, it means that love was no more than a means to get something. "I love me, therefore, I want you . . . If I cannot have you, then I despise you and want to hurt you."

If, on the other hand, one can, by means of the Holy Spirit, say, "I want the life of my beloved to be as full and as happy and as guilt-free as possible, because I love that person so," it is tantamount to picking up a cross. It's reminiscent of a prayer that read, "If it be possible . . . nevertheless, not as I will . . ."

If I love you best by giving you distance and space,
I shall give you distance and space.
If I love you best by rejoicing for you for your other affections,
I shall rejoice for you.
If I love you best by directing that love to other needs that surround me,
then that I shall do
—because I love you best, not me best.

What that does to the pain of brokenness is make of it an instrument of love. It makes my love a *verb* and thus rescues me from the feeling of helplessness, the feeling that there is nothing I can do. It is, so to speak, a way of sowing the grief, of investing the sorrow, of *doing* something positive with it; and in so doing, it becomes an action in which God can also have a hand.

I don't pretend to understand how God acts on our lives. I cannot believe that God guides and governs every accident and incident that occurs and that, therefore, we can simply turn to God to earn our living, or solve our problems, or protect us from harm on the highway. Neither do I believe that God is removed, disinterested, and uninvolved in the world's history or in our personal

63

lives. I have faith, and I have some evidence, that God can take the thread of any event and weave it into a pattern for our good in his own time, but that requires our faithful and patient cooperation. I believe this, even with respect to the torturous agonies of broken loves. We have experienced them and we shall experience others, but C. S. Lewis was right that "to love at all is to be vulnerable."

The whole of what Lewis said is this:

> Love anything, and your heart will certainly be wrung and possibly be broken. If you want to make sure of keeping it intact, you must give your heart to no one, not even to an animal. Wrap it carefully round with hobbies and little luxuries; avoid all entanglements; lock it up safe in the casket . . . safe, dark, motionless, airless . . . It will not be broken; it will become unbreakable, impenetrable, irredeemable.[1]

That, to me, and I suspect to all of us, would be slow death. No one is safer than a dead person, and no one is deader than a person who is safe. I'd rather be vulnerable and take my chances. Real love is only for those who are willing to take the risks of love in the confidence that all of our loves are kept and finally redeemed in the love of God.

NINE

If Jesus Had Died in Bed

Scripture: Romans 5:1-8

IT'S TRUE, you know, that Jesus would not have had to die the way he did. Instead of dying the humiliating death of a common criminal, he could have lived a good long time, teaching and preaching like rabbis before him, telling stories, quoting Scripture, and dying finally of old age, perhaps in bed.

Of course, in order to die differently, he would have had to live differently. He'd have had to stop preaching the supremacy of love over the law. He'd have had to forget the foolishness of unlimited forgiveness. He'd have had to choose his company a bit more carefully instead of devoting so much of his attention to the lower rungs of the social ladder. He would certainly have had to give up criticizing the established religious and social order in and out of the synagogue, declaring how they violated the will of God. In other words, if he'd been willing to do more "comforting of the disquieted" and less "disquieting of the comfortable," he'd have lived longer.

And what if he had? What if, instead of a limited three-year ministry ending in public execution, he had preached and taught for thirty years and died in bed?

To start with, I wouldn't be writing this, and you wouldn't be reading it. There wouldn't be a Salvation Army and thousands of agencies like it around the world. There would probably be orphanages or homes for troubled youth, but one wonders what they would be like

65

and how they would have come about, because the church of Jesus Christ was the first to build those that now exist. There would be hospitals, no doubt, but the church was the first to provide those institutions for all who needed them. The church was even the first to build colleges and universities in this country.

You see, I believe that the assumption that we have caring responsibilities for our neighbors, no matter who they are and regardless of their ability to repay us, comes directly from Jesus. But it does not come just from what Jesus *taught*. And it would not have penetrated twenty centuries of time if Jesus had just taught thirty more years and died comfortably at sixty-five.

Let me explain that, because I think many Christians miss this point! I hear people talk sometimes as though the most important thing about Jesus is his teachings. I don't believe this. As great as his teachings were, they were not the most important thing about Jesus. Most of what Jesus said has its parallels in other rabbinic sayings. His two great commandments, love God and love your neighbor as yourself, were taken right out of the Old Testament.

Nor is it the fact that he died for what he believed. Many others have died on the field of battle in our own time to defend high causes and traditions. There were great men of antiquity, like Socrates, who took their own lives rather than deny their convictions. There are thousands of people around the world at this very moment who are being imprisoned, tortured, and killed for their fidelity to their political or religious beliefs. The fathers or husbands or sons of some of you, and some daughters, too, have died for their love for and faith in our country. Martyrdom is important, but it's not the most important thing about Jesus.

What is it then, more than just what Jesus said, or the way he treated people, or even the fact that he died rather than run away, that has caused him to change the shape of history and causes millions around the world of all races to find a common bond of hope and purpose? To discover the answer to that, think of the difference it would have made to all of us if, instead of dying upon the cross, Jesus had died in bed.

In scripture, Paul refers to us as sinners. That's a much-used word in the New Testament, but not a very popular one with us. We'll admit we are not perfect, that we are sometimes mistaken, or immature, but we do not like to say we are sinners.

I am absolutely convinced that one thing we would not know if Jesus had simply died in bed is just how deep and serious is this condition we call sin. We are so misled when we think of sin in terms of "bad things done." Sin is a condition, and one result of that condition is doing some things that are cruel to others, that are an injustice to ourselves and a violation of God. Sin is a condition that is basic, fundamental, deep in our nature: theologians would say, "original." And what is that original condition? What is "original sin"?

William Temple, onetime archbishop of Canterbury, explains it this way:

When we open our eyes as babies, we see the world stretching out around us; we are in the middle of it; all proportions and perspectives in what we see are determined by the relation—distance, height and so forth—of various visible objects to ourselves. This will remain true of our bodily vision for as long as we live. I am the center of the world I see; where the horizon is depends upon where I stand. Now, just the same thing is true at first of our mental and spiritual vision. Some things please

67

us; we hope they will happen again; we call them good. Our standard of values is the way things affect ourselves. So each of us takes his place at the center of his own world.

But I am not the center of the world or the standard of reference between good and bad. I am not, and God is. In other words, from the beginning I put myself in God's place. This is my original sin. I was doing it before I could speak and everyone else has been doing it from early infancy. I am not "guilty" on this account because I could not help it. But I am in a state, from birth, in which I shall bring disaster on myself and everyone affected by my conduct unless I can escape from it.[1]

You get the image? We don't have to think very long in order to see how that spells out in our own lives. When we bump heads with someone, it's our own head we hold. Our attention is on ourselves most of the time. Our "self-consciousness" stands in the way of our awareness of others. Our selfishness interferes with our generosity. Our pride, our defensiveness, and our greed move us to unspeakably cruel behavior sometimes, as persons and as a nation of persons. That's when our sinful condition expresses itself in sinful behavior.

Perhaps the most graphic illustration of this is how humanity treated Jesus in Jerusalem in his last week. The story dramatizes what the rest of us have been doing to him and those like him ever since.

Jesus was not just Jesus; he was also Christ. He was "of God." And yet, the very people who hailed his coming with palm branches kept a cautious silence at the time of his trial. Leo Tolstoy tells a story of an onlooker at the scene of the crucifixion, who scarcely paid any attention to what was happening to Jesus because he had such a nagging toothache of his own.

This painful revelation, so like myself, would probably never have been made known as forcefully to me if Jesus had died in bed. It's one thing for us to be cruel to someone who is mean, or cruel to someone who is indifferent; but to be cruel to a man who loves us and would give his life for us, shows us just how cruel and selfish and sinful we can be. It takes the vision of Jesus on the cross to make us see ourselves as we are.

But there is a greater and more amazing knowledge than this, and that has to do with how God responds to this fact of my sinfulness. For the truth is that God would have every right to condemn and reject me for the attitude I have persisted in taking toward him and toward his human family so often. God is certainly under no obligation to make things right with me. And this is what utterly amazes me: God has every reason to let me suffer the consequences of my own selfish sinfulness—every reason, that is, except one, and that is God's great love for me. It is a love as great as if I were the only child God had.

Jesus taught about this when he told the parable of the Prodigal Son. But all the teaching Jesus ever did or could do in thirty or forty or fifty more years could not have persuaded me that God loves me like that. I would have continued to believe that there was some "fine print" somewhere, some qualifying clause in God's love which said—as the Old Testament said—that God loves me *when,* or *if,* or *unless,* or *until,* not just "God loves me"—without qualification, without end. I would not—could not—know that as I do, if Jesus had died in bed. Somehow there had to be sacrifice, not my sacrifice, but God's own sacrifice—the offering, so to speak, of God's own son.

So Jesus died on the cross to demonstrate to us how much God really loves us. Thus does Paul write, "While we were still weak, at the right time Christ died for the ungodly. Why, one will hardly die for a righteous man—though perhaps for a good man one will dare even to die. But God shows his love for us in that while we were yet sinners Christ died for us" (Rom. 5:6-8).

That's why Jesus' crucifixion was a whole different order of death than the noble death of Socrates, for example; for while the Greek philosopher took the honorable death of a cup of hemlock for the sake of a principle, Jesus suffered humiliating execution for the sake of people—the very people who were crucifying him, which would have included me if I had been there.

Many have gone down fighting. But there's one thing even greater, and that is to go down loving. This Jesus did, permitting himself to suffer the things from which he could have escaped had he willed, enduring every suffering, struggling step of the way, expressing no malice at any point, and dying with a prayer of forgiveness upon his lips.

Thus this mysterious love of God becomes so very logical. It can change people—the Bible says, "save people" from their own willful, life-draining selfishness. This love can save the world. It is the only thing that can.

But Jesus, as great as he was and taught and lived, could never have revealed this to us so conclusively had he simply died in bed. He had to die just as he did for us to know that God's love runs deepest for those who deserve it the least.

Which leaves us with one more thing we know, which we would not know if Jesus had died in an easier, less dramatic way; and that is, how far God expects us to go with our loving. There may have been a question at one time; there is no question any more. The terror on Calvary was not just a historical event to be read about and remembered. The reason that this event has changed all history is that it has made its imprint on every succeeding generation of civilization.

G. A. Studdert-Kennedy said that ever since a certain time, when the meaning of Calvary was made especially real to him, he could never again see the world as anything but a crucifix: "I see the cross set up in every slum, in every filthy, overcrowded quarter, in every vulgar flaring street that speaks of luxury and waste of life. I see him staring up at me from the pages of a newspaper that tells of a tortured, lost, bewildered world."

It is before this cross that the followers of Jesus gather, week after week, not just to learn and recall what he did and what he taught, but to absorb and marvel at what God did in him: to be reminded that "God so loved the world that he gave his only Son, that whoever believes in him should not perish but have eternal life" (John 3:16). So we are called, you and I, to address the world with that same kind of love. That's why churches take offerings; that's why you and I may do some of the giving we do, spending ourselves on neighbors close at hand as well as on people we'll never know. Because that's what God calls us to do.

We have a condition we call sin, and God has a nature we call gracious love, and I have a calling—as do you—we call commitment.

If we did not know these things we would either ignore our guilt and destroy each other in our selfishness, or we would remain forever weighed down by hopeless remorse. We have been rescued—redeemed—from both of these terrible fates. I doubt we would have known this if Jesus had died in bed.

Ten

Being Born Under the Sign of Avis

Scripture: 1 Corinthians 3:10-23

A BOY in my church was once in a friendly foot-race with his four-year-old sister. Noting that she was having a hard time keeping up, he shouted out, "Second one there wins!" I thought, if ever there was a sound New Testament idea, that is it.

I call this sermon "Being Born Under the Sign of Avis." That's an altogether new astrological sign, taken from the car rental agency and referring to those of us who were born to be number two, though we may try harder. The patron saint of this sign of the zodiac is, of course, Charlie Brown. I suppose this is one reason we appreciate him so much. We recognize so much of him in ourselves that we can't help sympathizing. So I want to share these words with those who seem, no matter how hard we try, to come in second. And I want to proclaim that sometimes the second one there wins!

As I scan the New Testament, I'm at a loss to find anyone who quite parallels Charlie Brown, but the New Testament does give us some images of what I call the "Avis Syndrome." For example, there was Joseph, called Barsabbas, surnamed Justus. You all remember him, of course . . . You don't all remember him. That's what I mean. People born under the sign of Avis are not remembered.

Well, Joseph—called Barsabbas, surnamed Justus—was one of the two men brought forth to fill the vacancy left by Judas Iscariot after the betrayal. The other was

Matthias. As the book of Acts tells us, the disciples prayed and said, "Lord, who knowest the hearts of all men, show which one of these two thou hast chosen to take the place in this ministry and apostleship from which Judas turned aside, to go to his own place." And they cast lots for them, and the lot fell on Matthias, and he was enrolled with the eleven disciples (1:23-26). So with the flip of a coin, Matthias won, and Joseph called Barsabbas was *number two* and never heard from again.

Not as obvious a candidate for the "Avis Award" was Paul himself. We might never have considered Paul in that category, but remember, he had never even been in on any of the action. Paul never knew Jesus, never heard him preach, was not present for the crucifixion. He was a latecomer. It was after a notable career as a prosecutor of Christians that he had a dramatic conversion experience, and from then on was the most energetic missionary for the Christian faith in the entire first-century church. But Paul never forgot that he was an outsider; much of his career and his writing was devoted to defending his authority as an apostle. I suspect he tried harder than any of the others, but he never made *number one*.

Well, there are more obvious Avis contenders in the Bible. There was Zacchaeus, a born loser if ever there was one, whom everyone despised. Yet Jesus chose his home to go to for dinner! Then there was "that Mary," who was loved by several men, all in the same way. But Jesus got close to her and made her better than second class. In fact, Jesus seemed to spend a good deal of his time with number-two types, which takes me to the first point I want to make, and that has to do with how God feels about Charlie Brown and the rest of us.

Jesus spent a disproportionate amount of time with these people, bestowing love on them. Jesus didn't just speak to them in passing; he sought them out. He'd meet them at the well where everyone could see. He preached to them, but he also listened, which is much harder and much more important. For these were the unsuccessful ones, to whom no one listened.

So Jesus listened to them as no one else listened, because God listens. He not only listened to them, he called them to follow him. Jesus' whole first-string team was composed of number two types. In being called, they began to get the notion that they were as acceptable as the prizewinners, that God's love is not meted according to achievement or measured by awards.

This knowledge, when it penetrates beyond our brains and into our hearts, is the beginning of the meaning of salvation by grace. To people who know this experience or this reality, salvation is, at least in part, a very discernible, almost psychologically measurable transformation. And we all need transformation, not into someone else, but into our real selves.

It's normal enough to want to be well-liked, successful, to be laughed with and not laughed at, to be tolerably well-respected, certainly to be trusted and to make a positive difference to people. A person who really didn't care about these things would be a rare one indeed. When we are turned down, when our ratings drop or we make a poor commission some month, it bothers us. Sometimes poor income doesn't bother us as much as poor relations—the feeling that we are just not making it with people, not accepted, not sought out. It's normal for that to bother us.

The late Charles R. Brown (a different Charlie Brown, paradoxically) has observed that there are some people in every generation who are born with exceptional ability. He calls them four-leaf clovers in the field of life. But he points out, the clover that feeds the cows and bees and keeps the fields green is the ordinary, three-leaf clover. Most of the work of the world is done, not by those few four-leaf clovers, but by the common ordinary folks like you and me, who do the best we can with what we have.

The vast majority of people God ever created were of the three-leaf clover variety. To accept God's creation in grateful trust, which includes God's creation of us as we are, is one expression of our faith.

To refuse to do this, to accept ourselves only conditionally, is to be faithless to God. It's as if to say, "When it came to me, God, you really goofed!" That's an insult to God. God doesn't "goof," not in your creation nor in mine. God creates us unfinished, but what God creates, as the book of Genesis says, is "very good."

We are discussing a theological problem now—a problem of misunderstanding and mistrusting God—and consequently misunderstanding and discounting ourselves, which results from a misfocus on exceptional performances and exceptional personalities instead of upon the exceptional persons that each of us is, underneath our occasional aberrational behavior.

We recall the famous Jewish tale about Zusya, who was sad because he knew that in the last day, Jehovah would not ask him, "Zusya, why were you not Jeremiah?" or, "Zusya, why were you not Moses?" but rather, "Zusya, why were you not Zusya!"

It's no cinch to discover and be yourself in a society that is forever telling you how to dress, how to smell, what to think, what to do; a society that stresses competition and lays a heavy emphasis on achievement. America and Americans have always made a big thing out of being "number one." The implication is that everyone ought to be a four-leaf clover; and since that is not possible, it is little wonder some of us resort to self-recrimination, which sometimes makes us seek phony highs, or overachievement, or incessant wandering, or even suicide. And it doesn't need to be that way at all.

Jesus said, "No one can serve two masters." You will either be who society taunts you to be, or who God wants you to be—which introduces us to the final question. One way to put it is, "Who says Avis is number two, anyway?" Well, Hertz says it, as if that is what really counted. The world is not really the final authority on what constitutes number one. For all the world knows, sometimes the second one there wins!

I think of a young woman with an uncertain education, brought up in an orphanage, certainly no beauty to look at, and so near-sighted that she had to wear special glasses. Charlie Brown personified? Maybe. "Of questionable success as a private tutor," some said of Anne Sullivan, who became the teacher of Helen Keller. I suspect she never knew she was number one, and possibly never cared.

In the seventeenth century, a young lad by the name of Nicholas Herman, converted at the age of eighteen, wanted desperately to become part of a leading monastery, yearned to be a scholar. But everyone thought him to be too unlearned to be with the real scholars, so they put him in the kitchen. And there he stayed, simply writing letters and talking with people from time to time. But ever since some of those letters and conversations were published, Nicholas Herman, or Brother Lawrence, as he was called, has been one of the most sought-after mystics in all of Christian history. I guess he never did make number one as a scholar, but God had his own rating system, with which the world only much later caught up.

As long as I have mentioned Paul, let me make clear that being number one with the Jerusalem church was not his ambition—but it was his ambition to be on the straight and level with his Lord. And so he reminds us: "Let no one deceive himself. If any one among you thinks that he is wise in this age, let him become a fool that he may become wise. . . . So let no one boast of men. For all things are yours, whether Paul or Apollos or Cephas or the world or life or death or the present or the future, all are yours; and you are Christ's; and Christ is God's" (1 Corinthians 3:18, 21-23).

One final illustration to caution us from assuming we know so much about who's first and second. Reread these words from Matthew 27:15-23:

> Now at the feast the governor was accustomed to release for the crowd any one prisoner whom they wanted. And they had then a notorious prisoner, called Barabbas. So when they gathered, Pilate said to them, "Whom do you want me to release for you, Barabbas or Jesus who is called Christ?" For he knew that it was out of envy that they had delivered him up. Besides, while he was sitting on the judgment seat, his wife sent word to him, "Have nothing to do with that righteous man, for I have suffered much over him today in a dream." Now the chief priests and the elders persuaded the people to ask for Barabbas and destroy Jesus. The governor again said to them, "Which of the two do you want me to release for you?" And they said, "Barabbas." Pilate said to them, "Then what shall I do with Jesus who is called Christ?" They all said, "Let him be crucified." And he said, "Why, what evil has he done?" But they shouted all the more, "Let him be crucified."

Born under the sign of Avis, or so it would appear. At that point, Barabbas appeared to be the winner. It was much too early to tell that the second one won. Hence a lesson to remember, though you forget all else written here: a sentence I once heard a man speak at a time I needed most to hear it, and one that is still easier for me to say than to remember: "God does not call us to be successful; only faithful."

ELEVEN

What Jesus Couldn't Tell Us

Scripture: Ecclesiastes 1:1-11;
John 16:1-12

"I HAVE yet many things to say to you, but you cannot bear them now."

I suppose it's really anybody's guess what Jesus had in mind when he spoke those mysterious words as recorded in John 16:12. We all know, of course, that the gospels don't give us a complete record of everything Jesus said and did. As a matter of fact, our record is amazingly sketchy. But here he says he had other things to say, but his disciples, meaning us, couldn't bear them, which indicates that even if some ancient stenographer had carefully recorded all of Jesus' words, there was still more that went unsaid. Have you ever wondered what those things were? I cannot pretend to know with certainty to what Jesus was referring, but two or three possibilities come to mind.

First, let's be clear that Jesus wasn't holding anything back with regard to the costs of discipleship. He laid it on the line pretty well when he said, "They will put you out of the synagogues; indeed, the hour is coming when whoever kills you will think he is offering service to God" (John 16:2). This language makes it clear that to follow Jesus is no spring outing, and Jesus did not hesitate a minute to make sure his listeners were clear on that. For it would not have been fair to have given the impression— an impression that, unfortunately, is given sometimes in our day—that the Christian life is not only a punched

78

ticket to heaven, but a guarantee of success and happiness on earth: that if you just mix a little Christianity along with everything else, life will be just fine.

But Jesus was not calling us to *another* commitment. He was calling us to *the* commitment, the commitment to which all other commitments come second, and from which all other commitments derive their deepest meaning. But take this commitment seriously, says Jesus, and you are not only seeking salvation, you are asking for trouble. You may ask for comfort and for strength, but you cannot ask for safety. You can drink deeply of the joys of the world, but you cannot turn your back on the problems of the world.

All this Jesus made clear many times over, so it certainly wasn't those words we could not bear to hear. We may not have listened, but we *have* heard the words.

Perhaps what he could not tell us was that progress in our lives and in the life of the world would sometimes be distressingly slow, that even with the self-sacrifice of devoted followers by the thousands, human society might plod on for decades or even for centuries without showing much evidence of improvement. This he left unsaid, knowing that we could not bear those tidings.

I agree that his earliest followers, willing as they became to live the Master's way and to seal it with the offering of their own lives, could not have withstood being told that the immediate fruits of their sacrifices would be unnoticeable. Such a prediction might well have been just enough to sap them of any enthusiasm they might have had for following Jesus.

Today we are far enough away from the time in which Jesus said those words that we can view human history and see that it has been a slow course, a halting, up-and-down course that has left in its wake many who are convinced that no progress has been made at all. One time, Dostoevski wrote, "The only contribution which

79

civilization has made is to increase man's capacity for pain." And Max Weber once characterized the movement of history during the past several centuries as "the progressive disenchantment with the world." How many are there whom you and I encounter who sincerely believe that the human race is worse off than it ever was, and that Christ and his church have had no significant effect upon civilization, except, perhaps, in the fields of art and architecture, music and poetry? There are times, I suppose, when all of us wonder about this. We are tempted to say, as Eve Curie did while looking down over Jerusalem:

> Oh, Jesus: you told us to be kind and forgiving, but for twenty solid centuries, wretched, incorrigible men have gone on being merciless, full of violence and of hatred. Religious men and atheists alike have lived and ruled in an unchristian way, and look at us now: we've never been in a worse mess.[1]

I can see how we could get into those moods. On all levels of human problems, from personal to international, "it's a hard game," and it gets discouraging. Hence the words of "the preacher" from the Old Testament: "Vanity of vanities! All is vanity. . . . A generation goes, and a generation comes. . . . and there is nothing new under the sun" (Eccles. 1:2, 4, 9).

I'll tell you the words in that somber poem that get to me: "There is no remembrance of former things." When you see our country and others repeating some of the same mistakes we have made before, you start to wonder how long it takes us to learn from history. When you consider how you and I individually continue in habits and patterns that we strongly suspect are destructive, yet we continue, it is as if, indeed, "there is no remembrance."

Actually, it isn't as hopeless as we sometimes feel, nor as Ecclesiastes makes it sound. I believe the human race—agonizingly slowly, to be sure—is growing up. There is a story of a reincarnated king of Babylon, visiting one of our modern cities. His host and guide undertook to show him the sights of the city. He made rounds of the brothels, the gambling joints, the opium dens, the taverns, the hideouts for gangsters, and the like. The king was polite but bored. He said, "We had all these in Babylon three thousand years ago, and on the whole, we did it better. Have you nothing new to show me?" So his guide reversed his field and took his guest to day care centers, libraries, schools and hospitals, public health centers, research laboratories, transient centers, soup kitchens, and institutions for the disabled. "Ah," said the king, "all this is new. We didn't have *these* things in Babylon."

Sometimes we see our whole nation rivet its attention to the plight of a single child whose life hangs in the balance, which shows us something about the compassionate capabilities of the human race that once were not so evident. The massive rallying around of people to provide food for the starving of Africa is the kind of compassion I don't recall being reported a few centuries ago. You cannot convince me that the Christian story, from manger to cross, with all its implications as to how human life is meant to be lived, has not had its impact on the world.

I believe that if the earliest followers of Jesus could look upon the world in our age, on the whole they would be encouraged by many changes they see. What would discourage them utterly would be the discovery that it took two thousand years for us to get this far. Perhaps Jesus knew that his followers could not bear to be told that their greatest efforts would show so little immediate effect on humanity. It still feels that way; yet you and I as individuals have more potential for impact than persons in any previous age or society.

But that may not have been at all what Jesus had in

mind when he spoke those words to his disciples. Perhaps it was that, as much as they would feel forsaken by their friends, they would also feel forsaken by God. The pressures would sometimes be so great, the fruits so little, that it would seem as if God had forgotten them, and *that* they could not bear to hear.

Instead of dwelling on this at any length, Jesus simply assured them of his continuing presence, of their oneness with God, and the necessity of their utter dependence on him, come what may. Jesus wasn't ignoring the problem. He knew all too well of his own "dark nights of the soul," and we know that among his own last words was his agonizing cry to a God he felt had forsaken him. Perhaps Jesus knew his disciples couldn't bear to be told that there would be such times. He knew their experience would reveal it to them. The Spirit of truth would make it known.

But Jesus also knew that the Spirit of truth would reveal that beyond such feelings of estrangement will be, for those who seek it, a deeper sense of companionship than ever before. For when, in our loneliness, we become desperate for God's presence and help, then we will find it. When, in our weakness, we acknowledge our need for God's strength; when, in our aimlessness, we acknowledge our need for God's direction; when, in our sin, we acknowledge our need for God's forgiveness: *then,* in our willingness to have God near, do we discover God *is* near and, in fact, has never left us.

Someone has said, "If you don't feel as close to God as you once did, guess who moved?" God wants to share in our struggles. At the very points where we feel we deserve him least, then do we need him most, and then does God yearn most to help.

Perhaps Jesus couldn't tell his disciples of the feeling of forsakenness by God that he himself had felt and that they would feel. They were not ready for that. It probably would have no meaning for them as yet. But it would be revealed to them, and it would also be revealed that through just such experiences does one's faith really come of age.

Of course, that may not be at all what Jesus felt he could not tell them. It might have been something quite different from any of these things. For example, we note throughout the New Testament how incomplete his answers were in regard to the life to come. What happens after death? He gives us hints; he suggests some trials in this life from which we shall be wonderfully free in the life to come, and he also suggests that the most abiding values in this life continue—the values of love and companionship. But beyond this, he does not say.

I know that the later Christians have painted very graphic visions of this new life, as a four-cornered city with golden streets, which is neither more nor less than an effort to explain that it is the nicest kind of existence we can imagine. But that vision is imperfect, simply because a four-cornered city with golden streets is not everybody's idea of heaven. I believe Jesus could have told us more than he did about this had he really wanted to. But he stopped short of revealing more because he didn't feel we could handle it—and for good reason. If we knew more exactly what lay ahead for those who prepare for it, all of our attention would be drawn from this life to the next. We would establish right relations with people and refrain from doing injustice to them, not for the sake of people, but for the sake of the reward we might receive. We would be so impressed by the life to come that we would lose all motivation to improve this world, to seek to establish God's will on earth as it is in heaven.

There is a real possibility that if we could get a clear glimpse of what is to come, we would lose most of our interest in living our present life. And that would utterly defeat the purpose of this life, which is, among other things, a proving ground for our faith, a laboratory for loving. This doesn't mean that all this life is for is to prepare us for the next one. God delivered us from that shallow view of living. What it does mean is that this life is *part* of the next—that the love which is in the very atmosphere of the next life begins here, in our relationships: that our companionship with God, which is the very substance of heaven, has its beginning here.

We will be prepared for heaven to the measure that we have developed our faith. This does not come about in the face of conclusive evidence, but rather in the midst of things hoped for and things unseen. We will be prepared for heaven to the measure that we are able to love, not just those whom it is easy to love, but all those who need our love—and those who need it most are the hardest to love of all.

In other words, our attention dare not be distracted from this life to the next, lest we lose all motive to live and grow and labor and love here and now. We have the assurance that this is not all, and that the quality of this life has a bearing on the quality of the next. If we had more evidence than this, it would defeat life's purpose, God's purpose. And so, Jesus couldn't tell us.

Of course, it may not have been this either, or any of the things I've mentioned, that was in Jesus' mind when he said, "I have yet many things to say to you, but you cannot bear them now" (John 16:12). The truth is, I don't know for sure. What I do know, is that I don't feel in the least bit cheated by what Jesus didn't tell us, for I am persuaded that as little as we know, and as much as he may have left unsaid, his word and his life tell me everything I need to know about abundant and purposeful and eternal living—in other words, about salvation from shallow, purposeless, limited living.

I do not need to be told more. I need to do more about what Jesus has already told me.

TWELVE

The Master's Touch

Scripture: Psalm 3;
Mark 5:24-34

BEFORE THE coming of Jesus nearly two thousand years ago, one of the popular notions of the coming Messiah within Judaism was something akin to a knight on a white charger who would slay the foes of the Jews and set the chosen people upon the throne of the world. It was rather like the hope expressed in the Third Psalm:

Arise, O Lord!
    Deliver me, O my God!
For thou dost smite all my enemies on the cheek,
thou dost break the teeth of the wicked.

Little wonder that in the coming of Jesus, whom many called the Messiah, there was considerable bewilderment—even disappointment—because Jesus just did not fit the picture that many had in mind. His method was not the predicted method at all; for instead of a knight on a white charger came a quiet and humble lover of people—carpenter by trade, preacher by avocation.

John the Baptist, in his disappointment over not seeing more dramatic action, sends word from prison to Jesus: "Are you he who is to come, or shall we look for another?" (Matthew 11:2). It's the same question we hear today, born of the same frustration that Christ and his church don't seem to forceably bring justice into the world, don't right a lot of wrongs, "break the teeth of the

85

wicked," or even produce a community of especially good people. Is Jesus the one after all, or should we look for another?

Jesus' answer to John then is his answer to us now: "Tell John what you hear and see: the blind receive their sight and the lame walk, lepers are cleansed and the deaf hear, and the dead are raised up, and the poor have good news preached to them" (Matt. 11:4-5). It was as if he were saying, "My style—God's style—is not a violent revolution, but a firm and gentle touch upon the hearts of people." Ever since that time, there have been many who have wanted to know more about the mystery of the Master's touch, which so often brought health to the sick, strength to the weak, direction to the lost, and light to those dark nights of the soul.

We want to know more about this Master's touch, not only because of our own need to be touched like that (or perhaps our remembrance of having been touched like that), but because of our willingness to touch others in this way. For we are called not just to watch, but to follow. We are asked not just to *like* Jesus, but to *be like* Jesus. I believe one reason we gather in church week after week is not just to receive the Master's touch, but to renew our willingness and ability to touch the way the Master touched.

Scripture tells us about the woman who had been sick for many years and had tried all the physicians she knew, but to no avail. And then she heard about Jesus. So when he came to her town, she joined the throng that gathered to see him, in hopes, perhaps, to talk to him. But the crowd was large and she was shy; and as Jesus moved along, the movement of the throng threatened to separate them, so that she would not even be close enough to reach out to him. So she "came up behind him in the crowd and touched his garment. For she said, 'If I touch even his garments, I shall be made well'" (Mark 5:27-28).

Then something happened that took her by surprise. Her hemorrhage stopped. Actually, she expected that. What surprised her, and everyone else, was that Jesus stopped in the midst of his brisk pace—stopped and turned and asked, "Who touched my garments?" The disciples were perplexed, as it seems they almost always were. "You see the crowd pressing around you, and yet you say, 'Who touched me?'" (For the past quarter of a mile, he had been well-touched!)

But Jesus, knowing that a crowd is still made up of persons, looked around to see who had done it. Scripture says the woman was frightened; she came in fear and trembling. Who wouldn't be frightened to have all eyes focused on you, as certainly they were upon her when Jesus gazed at her and her alone in the midst of the crowd.

She was frightened, but she came and she had that hoped-for conversation. She "fell down before him, and told him the whole truth." Before they parted, Jesus said, "Daughter, your faith has made you well; go in peace, and be healed of your disease."

It all sounds like an account of someone touching Jesus, but it was more than that. It is one of a whole series of accounts of Jesus' touch on people—people unsure of their worth, people feeling guilty about their lives, people feeling out of touch with others and with reality and with God: people, therefore, with all kinds of ailments.

Jesus won an early reputation for being a faith-healer, for healing the lame and the deaf and the blind and the leprous. So easy was it for him to win that kind of reputation that he frequently told people not to tell others what had happened to them—because his touch had an effect much deeper than the physical healing.

When Jesus sent word back to John the Baptist, listing the various kinds of healing episodes, he concluded by saying, "And the poor have good news preached to them." Those words have always struck me as something of an anticlimax, as if nothing practical was done for poor people but to tell them to cheer up. In Isaiah, which Jesus read from the pulpit of his hometown synagogue, the good news had to do with the justice that would be done. (61:1 ff.).

Jesus speaks in the New Testament not simply of the poverty-stricken, but of the poor in spirit, which really included about everybody. In addition, the "poor" included women, who were generally considered to be second-class humans. The Jews had written a prayer, "Blessed are Thou, O Lord, who hast not made me a woman." But the touch of Jesus disclosed that women mattered—even Samaritan women—and were no less the objects of God's love than the men themselves. This was a revolutionary idea.

The "poor" included children, whom even the disciples tried to keep from Jesus because they were a nuisance. And in a day when babies were sometimes left to die of exposure, especially if they were girl babies, Jesus' touch was more revolutionary than we realize, for he lifted up a child in the midst of the crowd and said, "Unless you turn and become like children, you will never enter the kingdom of heaven" (Matt. 18:3).

And the "poor" included the leftovers of society, the people on whom everyone else looked down. So Jesus picked that despicable little runt Zacchaeus out of a tree for his private dining companion. He tapped the shoulder of Matthew, that tax collector, despised as were all tax collectors, and said, "Follow me," making him one of the first of the twelve disciples. He did the same to Judas, which reminds us of the risks involved in trust.

Jesus touched people, sometimes with his hands, sometimes only with his eyes or the tone of his voice. That woman with a hemorrhage touched the garment of Jesus, but by the time the episode was over, he had touched her in a manner that enabled her to know that she really existed, that she really was somebody; and with that new confidence, that new faith, she was made whole by the affirming love of God. That's the Good News, preached in word and deed to the poor of that day and of our own.

We, as Christians, are called to imitate Jesus' style, paralleling his manner and cultivating his touch. It is not easy to do, and we should not mislead ourselves into thinking it is. For the style and manner of Jesus is radically different from the style we usually exalt, nationally and personally. Our style is more customarily that of the Third Psalm, to regard those who differ from us or fear us or threaten us by smiting their cheeks and breaking their teeth. That style, which can make an individual pompous or a nation a bully, is often appealing to our pride, but over the long haul it is unproductive. Jesus said that and demonstrated it, to the dismay of those who wanted him to call down legions of angels to put his enemies in their place.

This may surprise you, but I'd like to share with you an inspiring statement by a Communist, by one of the world's first Communist political activists. His family name is Vladimir Ilyich Ulyanov. You and I know him as Nikolai Lenin. Late in 1921, he became ill, lost the power of speech, and was obliged to let others rule in his name. Among the things he wrote in that period were these remarkable words:

> I made a mistake. . . . Without doubt, an oppressed multitude had to be liberated. But our method only provoked further oppression and atrocious massacres. My living nightmare is to find myself lost in an ocean red with the blood of innumerable victims. It is too late now to alter the past, but what was needed to save Russia was ten Francis of Assisi's.

One doesn't often hear such a profound admission about the futility of violence. But before we settle into any self-satisfaction and say, "I told you so," we had better turn the question upon ourselves: "What style do *we* most idolize and emulate?" Only belatedly did Mahatma Gandhi become our hero. Only belatedly did Martin Luther King, Jr. become our hero, and only belatedly did Jesus Christ. Yet it was that Master's touch, according to Gandhi, that freed India. It was that Master's touch, according to King, that nonviolently broke the bonds of oppression and freed black and white alike in our country.

It is the same touch upon a nation or a person that can bring total transformation to a situation or to a life. And this is where we must begin, you and I, if we are to help God make a difference to the world: we must begin with the offering of ourselves. It requires the humility, the expectation, the persistence, and the faith of that woman who sought for Jesus in the crowd. "If I touch even his garments, I shall be made well." If you and I can but shed the trappings of selfish, plastic, aggressive values—leave vengeance to the Lord, as the psalmist says—and open ourselves to the touch of Christ, we will become new creatures.

Myra Brooks Welch's poem about the violin auctioneer expresses it well:

'Twas battered and scarred, and the auctioneer
Thought it scarcely worth his while
To waste much time on the old violin,
But he held it up with a smile:
"What am I bidden, good folks," he cried,
"Who'll start the bidding for me?"
"A dollar, a dollar," then, "Two." "Only two?"
"Two dollars and who'll make it three?"
"Three dollars once, three dollars twice:
Going for three, . . . " but no.
From the room far back, a gray haired man
Came forward and picked up the bow;

THE MASTER'S TOUCH

Then wiping the dust from the old violin
and tightening the loosened strings,
He played a melody pure and sweet
As a carolling angel sings.

The music ceased, and the auctioneer,
With a voice that was quiet and low,
Said, "What am I bid for the old violin?"
And he held it up with the bow.
"A thousand dollars." "And who'll make it two?
Two thousand. Who'll make it three?"
"Three thousand once, three thousand twice,
and going and gone," said he.
The people cheered, but some of them cried,
"We do not quite understand
What changed it's worth." Swift came the reply:
"The touch of the Master's hand."

And many a man with life out of tune,
And battered and scarred with sin,
Is auctioned cheap to the thoughtless crowd,
Much like the old violin.
A "mess of pottage, a glass of wine,"
A game—and he travels on.
He is "going" once and "going" twice.
He's "going" and almost "gone."
But the Master comes, and the foolish crowd
Can never quite understand
The worth of a soul and the change that's wrought
By the touch of the Master's hand.[1]

We do not have to be down and out to need that touch.
Pray God we may be so touched, and that we may then
touch the world around us and help to make it well.

NOTES

1. Why Jesus Never Had Ulcers

1. F. W. Faber, *Growth in Holiness* (London: T. Richardson & Son, 1872).

2. Prayer and a Rabbit's Foot

1. W. H. Auden, *For the Time Being, A Christmas Oratorio* (Cleveland & New York: World Publishing Co., *Religious Drama no. 7,* Meridian Living Age Books, 1957). Reprinted with permission of Random House.
2. Mark Twain, *The Adventures of Huckleberry Finn* (New York: W. W. Norton & Co., 1977).
3. Dean William Inge, *A Rustic Moralist* (New York: G. P. Putnam's Sons, 1937).

3. Is the Golden Rule Really Christian?

1. Edwin McNeill Poteat, "The Jericho Road," from *Over the Sea, the Sky* by Edwin McNeill Poteat. Copyright © 1945 by Harper & Row, Publishers, Inc. Reprinted by permission of Harper & Row, Publishers, Inc.

4. Why Do the Good Suffer?

1. Francis Thompson, "Hound of Heaven," *Masterpieces of Religious Verse,* ed. James Dalton Morrison (New York: Harper & Bros., 1948).

7. The Old Looking-up-in-the-air Trick

1. Carl Sandburg, slightly adapted and abridged from, "To a Contemporary Bunkshooter" in *Chicago Poems* by Carl Sandburg, Copyright © 1916 by Holt, Rinehart, and Winston, Inc.; Renewed 1944 by Carl Sandburg. Reprinted by permission of Harcourt, Brace, Jovanovich, Inc.